The Ultimate History of

Rock'n'Roll

Drumming

1948 - 2000

by Daniel Glass

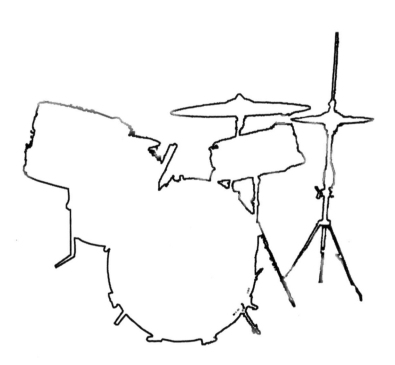

Acknowledgments/Credits:

Many thanks to Zoro and John Beck for their inspiration and support at the outset of this project. Thanks also to Steve Clark and Billy Vera for their thoughtful suggestions along the way, and to Mark Cally for his assistance with graphics and layout.

Very special thanks to Marcella Manzanedo for her love and support, and for putting up with my never-ending musical obsessions.

Front cover photo: Daniel Glass (the "model" was my red sparkle 1960 Rogers Holiday kit!)
Back cover photo: Christopher Kadish

About Daniel Glass:

A resident of Los Angeles, Daniel Glass has played drums for the pioneering "neo-swing" group Royal Crown Revue since 1994. He has also recorded and performed with Bette Midler, Freddy Cole, Al Viola, Mike Ness, Johnny Boyd, Debbie Davies, Unknown Hinson, Glen Glenn, Robert Gordon and many others. Daniel is the author of *The RCR Drum Transcription Book* as well as the forthcoming *Commandments of Roots Drumming* series. His writings on drum history have appeared in *Modern Drummer*, *DRUM!*, and *Stick It* magazines, and in various online publications like LA2nite.com, musician.com and learn2drum.com. To learn more about Daniel and his obsession with classic American music, please visit: www.danielglass.com.

Contents

Foreword

Although I'm known primarily as a jazz and swing drummer, I grew up an absolute rock'n'roll fanatic. One of my first musical memories - around the age of three or four - was hearing the Beatles' "Come Together" when it hit number one on "American Top Forty." At the age of eight, my best friend introduced me to harder-edged stuff like Deep Purple, Aerosmith, Black Sabbath, and Pink Floyd. That's when I really got hooked. Deep Purple's Ian Paice became my hero, and when I got my first drum kit a couple of years later, I had no qualms about setting up lefty - because that's how Ian did it.

Throughout the years, even as my own musical pursuits took me into different directions, I never stopped listening to rock, nor finding inspiration in it. When I joined Royal Crown Revue in 1994, the band actively encouraged me to bring a rock'n'roll intensity to the jazz and swing-inflected tunes we were writing. Combining rock with earlier musical eras helped give us a unique sound ("neo-swing") that spearheaded a musical movement in the 1990s, and allowed us to enjoy an incredibly diverse career that has stretched from international jazz festivals to punk rock tours.

The genesis for this book arose when I was contacted by John Beck, Percussion Chair at the Eastman School of Music in Rochester, NY. He had heard of my interest in drum history, and wanted me to write an entry on rock'n'roll drumming for the *Encyclopedia of Percussion*. Now, writing an encyclopedia entry on *anything* is intimidating enough. But rock'n'roll? That's like asking someone to write down everything there is to know about dogs . . . or space . . . or Bill Gates' bank account. Despite deep misgivings, I plunged in headfirst. The work was arduous to say the least. For three solid months, I dragged my computer literally everywhere - on tours of Japan and Australia, to social outings, even to the beach once or twice. Since I didn't want to leave anybody out, what began as an encyclopedia chapter eventually turned into the book you now hold in your hands.

I'm sure that various readers will take me to task for not including *their* favorite drummer, for spending more time on influential unknowns than million selling superstars, or including a different song/album than the one they feel best represents a particular player. Aside from the particulars, however, one thing is for sure: this book does manage to cover *a lot* of ground. I doubt you will find another single document that covers so many decades and sub-genres, and includes the names of so many important figures. Let's just say this is a good start.

One final note: In 1999, I finally got the chance to meet my childhood drum hero, Ian Paice, (he was playing at a major charity event in a band that included Paul McCartney and Pink Floyd guitarist David Gilmour – how cool is that!). In talking with Ian, I learned that – along with many of his peers from the 1960s British rock scene – he was first inspired by jazz players like Gene Krupa, Max Roach and Buddy Rich. We both had a good laugh when we realized that he - a rocker raised on jazz - had inspired me - a jazzer raised on rock! It's funny how things come full circle like that.

I hope you have as much fun reading this book as I did writing it!

Introduction

"Rock'n'Roll"

Probably the world's best-known three-word contraction, the term "rock'n'roll" has become such a part of our collective unconscious that it practically defies definition. We all know that rock'n'roll is a musical style, yet it has also come to represent an attitude, a feeling, even a way of life. The words themselves evoke images of anticipation, excitement, and unbridled joy. If we want to get the adrenaline flowing for an important or exhilarating activity, we pump ourselves up with the phrase "Let's rock'n'roll!" When we declare that someone or something "rocks," we have paid a compliment of the highest order. Rock'n'roll is not a phrase content to be merely uttered; it demands to be shouted!

If the words that we choose to describe rock'n'roll seem to carry a sexual connotation, it should come as little surprise. The term itself (like "jazz") derives from an African-American euphemism for lovemaking, and has been celebrated in blues derived music for nearly a century. Trixie Smith sang "My Man Rocks Me (With One Steady Roll)" back in 1922, and numerous other records celebrating the suggestive activities inherent in "rockin'" and "rollin'" were released during the eras of early jazz, swing and rhythm and blues, years before Chuck Berry or Elvis first sang a note or picked up a guitar.

So, if a song contains "rock'n'roll" in the title, does that necessarily make it a "rock'n'roll song"? Of course not. Rock'n'roll is a unique, definable style of music that developed at a particular time in history. If our goal here is to clarify the who, what and when of that development, it might be wise to heed the perspective of noted rock historian Dave Marsh:

> "It always struck me that trying to trace the origin [of the term rock'n'roll] was not only futile, but involved a basic misconception of the issue. The question is not when somebody first sang the phrase "rock'n'roll" (or something akin to it), but when did music first started *sounding* a different way, and affecting people the way rock has and does." (1)

Any attempt to answer that question must start with a discussion of rock'n'roll drumming, because it is when the *groove* started to affect people in a "different way" that the music itself began to embody the energy expressed in its moniker. In essence, the creation of rock's so-called "big beat" *is* the story of rock'n'roll.

5

Chapter One: Early Rock: 1948-1964

Rhythm and Blues: The Birth of the Backbeat

The rock'n'roll story begins with rhythm and blues, a style of music that was popular among African-Americans for about a decade starting in the late 1940s. A big part of r&b's attraction had to do with the stompin' backbeats that made it so eminently danceable. Defined as a forceful stroke (often a rim shot) played on beats two and four of a drum pattern, the backbeat had been part of the drummer's vocabulary since the earliest days of jazz. However, in previous eras, backbeats were limited to certain sections of a song as a means of building emotional tension. Conventional wisdom of the day maintained that too much backbeat could be intrusive, if not downright overbearing. According to drummer Louie Bellson, "There was always a feeling of two and four, but generally, a loud backbeat was not present when you played swing." (2)

Starting in the late 1940s, however, some rhythm and blues recordings began to feature a continuous backbeat that ran the entire length of an arrangement. "Good Rockin' Tonight," as recorded by blues shouter Wynonie Harris in 1948, is one such example. **Clarence "Bobby" Donaldson**'s backbeats are clearly audible from start to finish, supported by a chorus of gospel-style handclaps (another percussive device that had long been used in the black church). If any fears about using a continuous backbeat still lingered, "Good Rockin' Tonight" put them to rest. Dancers went crazy for the heavier groove, sending the record to number one on the r&b charts and keeping it a top seller for six solid months.

Other examples of early backbeat r&b include Jimmy Preston and the Prestonians "Rock the Joint" (1949, **Eddie Winters**), Fats Domino's "The Fat Man," (1950, **Earl Palmer**), and Jackie Branston and His Delta Cats' "Rocket 88" (1951, **Willie Sims**). The success of all these recordings - first among African-American r&b listeners, and then among wider audiences - indicated that the backbeat was the first harbinger of heavier sounds to come.

Pop Music in a Segregated America

If a drummer's backbeat was the kind of innovation that obviously affected people in a "rock'n'roll" kind of way, is it safe to say that r&b *was* rock'n'roll? That's a matter of opinion. The debate over rock'n'roll's origins has been hotly contested among music historians for quite some time, and it may never be conclusively settled. One might safely posit, however, that music is in a constant state of evolution, and as rock'n'roll did not fall out of the sky fully formed, there were some other key ingredients that would have to be contributed before rock could truly qualify as its own genre.

One must remember that in the late 1940s, rhythm and blues was a phenomenon still found almost solely within African-American communities, the reflection of a music industry that - like much of American society - was essentially segregated. Outside of a few exceptions like Duke Ellington, Louis Jordan and Nat King Cole, African-American musicians had extremely limited access to the airplay and distribution opportunities that were afforded their white counterparts. Major labels of the day like RCA/Victor and Columbia were generally uninterested in blues based styles, which for years had borne the label "race" music. They considered it too rough, raw and vulgar for "mainstream" (a.k.a. white) listeners. As a result, r&b artists were forced to exist in a "separate but not so equal" world. They generally released their recordings on small, independent labels, and often had to rely on informal distribution networks (like barbershops, grocery stores and other mom and pop outlets in America's black communities) in order to sell records. Despite these unfavorable odds, r&b and its precursor, jump blues, managed to thrive during the 1940s, mainly because African-Americans, who had benefited from the wartime economic boom, were now a viable demographic that could support its own music scene.

The Rise of the Teenager

Until the early 1950s, most of white America was totally unaware of the existence of r&b. The emergence of a new phenomenon known as the teenager, however, would change all that. With average household incomes on the rise, America's young people no longer had to enter the work force at a young age. For the first time in the country's history, an entire generation of adolescents was blessed with the leisure time to reflect on what it meant to exist somewhere between the carefree life of a child and the responsible world of an adult. As it became clear that a disposable income was part of teen life, advertisers began to focus more strongly on the new demographic, marketing an increasing array of products specifically toward young people.

One of those "products" was rhythm and blues. As early as 1950, white disc jockeys like Hunter Hancock and Dick "Huggy Boy" Hugg began playing r&b records on mainstream radio stations. They geared their pitch toward a younger audience, broadcasting live from "record hops" at high school gymnasiums, and promoting mixed-race r&b shows at places like L.A.'s Olympic Auditorium and Brooklyn's Paramount Theatre. The music was an easy sell. With its pounding rhythms and wild stage performances, r&b had a danceable feel that was instantly appealing. It belied the conformism demanded by Cold War America, and gave teenagers their own unique sense of identity. When the country's most popular r&b DJ Alan Freed rechristened his nationally syndicated radio program "The Big Rock'n'Roll Show" in 1954, he was essentially repackaging an established musical tradition, and selling it as the hot new music for teens. Rock'n'roll was born.

Seeing the economic potential of rock'n'roll, the major record labels showed a renewed interest, and started to sign white acts whose sound was in the r&b vein. The most important of these early white acts was Bill Haley. Haley (along with his band the Comets) would shortly be eclipsed by more popular singers like Elvis Presley, but in 1954, he provided the first taste of rock'n'roll for countless young Americans.

Haley had been signed to the major label Decca in 1952 based on regional hits he'd had with covers of r&b favorites like Jimmy Preston's "Rock the Joint." It was the Comets' 1954 classic "(We're Gonna) Rock Around the Clock," however, which put Haley and rock'n'roll on the map. "Rock Around the Clock" was the first rock song to hit number one on the pop charts, it was the title of the first rock'n'roll LP, and it was the first rock record to be used in a movie (the juvenile delinquent-themed "Blackboard Jungle"). To this day, it remains one of the all-time rock anthems. **Billy Gussack**, a swing-era session drummer, played on this and other Haley hits like "Thirteen Women" and "Mambo Rock." Although his playing did not include the consistent backbeats of r&b, Gussack's inspired swing feel (peppered with Gene Krupa-style fills) locked in beautifully with the slap bass, honkin' sax and shout vocals that comprised Haley's signature sound. Other important contributors to the Haley groove were swing legend **Cliff Leeman** ("R-O-C-K") and **Ralph Jones** ("See You Later Alligator").

The Move to Straight 8ths

The mid-fifties saw the introduction of another rhythmic innovation that would help to clearly define rock'n'roll as a unique style. That innovation involved a "flattening" of the shuffle pattern, which had dominated the pop music landscape for five decades. Previous forms of American pop music - from Ragtime and New Orleans jazz to Dixieland, swing, and r&b - all had their rhythmic foundation in the "swung" eighth note (another name for the shuffle pattern). Certain r&b musicians, however, found that by speeding up the 8/8 feel of a boogie-woogie groove, it was possible to "straighten out" the bouncy feel of the shuffle and create a relentless, driving "chuck-chuck-chuck" of eighth notes that is now the recognizable trademark of rock.

Interestingly, the move toward straight eighths did not originate with drummers, but with other instrumentalists, notably piano player Little Richard, and guitar players Chuck Berry and Bo Diddley. Drummer **Earl Palmer**, who played on many important early rock recordings - both in his hometown of New Orleans and in Los Angeles - offers fascinating insight into the development of the straight eighth groove:

" . . . the only reason I started playing what they come to call a rock-and-roll beat came from trying to match Little Richard's right hand. *Ding-ding-ding-ding!* Most everything I had done before was a slow shuffle or slow triplets. Fats Domino's early things were shuffles . . . But Little Richard moved from a shuffle to that straight eighth-note feeling. I don't know who played that way first, Richard or Chuck Berry. Even if Chuck Berry played straight eighths on the guitar, his band still played a shuffle behind him. But with Richard pounding the piano with all ten fingers, you couldn't so very well go against it. I did at first – on "Tutti Frutti" you can hear me playing a shuffle. Listening to it now, it's easy to hear that I should have been playing that rock beat." (3)

Although much of fifties rock'n'roll would retain the shuffle as its basis, the straight eighth feel became increasingly popular as the decade wore on. Earl Palmer was undoubtedly one of the first to master the new style. With Little Richard, his driving straight eighths lit up many chart-topping classics, including "Lucille," "Good Golly Miss Molly," "Long Tall Sally" and "The Girl Can't Help It." **Charles Connor**, another Crescent City drummer who was a member of Richard's touring band, the Upsetters, displayed a wicked straight eighth style on Richard's 1957 classic "Keep a' Knockin." In the 1970s, John Bonham duplicated Connor's introduction almost note for note on the Led Zeppelin classic "Rock'n'Roll."

Chuck Berry is another pioneer who laid the straight-eighth feel of rock over an r&b groove. Berry became an instant smash with teen audiences when he released "Maybellene" in 1955, and his two-minute anthems to cars, guitars and dancing on the likes of "Johnny B. Goode" and "Roll Over Beethoven" (not to mention his famous "duck-walk" strut) will always be associated with rock's birth. Interestingly, Berry's straight-eighth guitar strumming on both of these hits was backed by a *swung* shuffle pattern (provided by blues drumming ace **Fred Below**), creating an unusual "in-between" groove that has come to be associated with the fifties rock sound. That groove can be heard on numerous hits from the era, including Elvis Presley's "Jailhouse Rock," and Jerry Lee Lewis' "Whole Lotta Shakin' Going On."

Bo Diddley, Chuck Berry's lablemate at Chess records, blazed a rock trail all his own. For starters, Diddley built his own instruments and effects, revolutionizing the sound of the electric guitar in the process. His recordings were visionary, incorporating elements of surf, soul and boogaloo years before those styles were officially christened. Diddley also utilized his rhythm section - drummer **Clifton James** and maraca player **Jerome Green** - to create a straight eight style that was unlike anything that had come before it. Songs like "Hey Bo Diddley" and "Hush Your Mouth" (both from 1955) are thunderous, double-time romps so divergent from the r&b of the period that they appear to have been sent from outer space.

Perhaps Diddley's biggest contribution to rock was his incorporation of an African rhythm called the *juba*. With a similar construction to the latin *clave* pattern, the juba had long been a part of the American cultural fabric (as the basis of a children's game called the hambone, and as the playful musical knock "Shave and a haircut, two bits"). In Diddley's hands, this rhythm became the centerpiece of many rock classics, including "Bo Diddley" and "Who Do You Love." "The Bo Diddley Beat," as it has come to be known, influenced countless other rock artists, and has been featured over the years in an impressive array of hits, including: "Not Fade Away" (Buddy Holly, Rolling Stones), "Magic Carpet Ride" (Steppenwolf), "Willie & the Hand Jive" (Johnny Otis, Eric Clapton), "Man Smart, Woman Smarter" (The Grateful Dead, Robert Palmer), "I Want Candy" (The Strangeloves, Bow Wow Wow), and "Faith" (George Michael).

Rockabilly: Country Music Adds Drums

In addition to rhythm and blues, another major contributor to the sound of fifties rock'n'roll was a Southern style known as rockabilly. Rockabilly had its birth at Sun Records, the tiny Memphis-based label that introduced the world to Carl Perkins, Elvis Presley, Jerry Lee Lewis, Johnny Cash and Roy Orbison, among many others.

Sun founder Sam Phillips was a huge fan of black music, and he had devoted the early years of his career to recording Southern r&b artists. Blues legends like Howlin' Wolf, B.B. King and Junior Parker all cut some of their first tracks with Sam Phillips. Ironically, although he appreciated the importance of backbeats in r&b, Phillips was *not* a fan of drums in *country* music. In fact, it was the general consensus among those in the country music industry that drums corrupted the acoustic origins of the music. As a result, Sun's earliest rockabilly recordings are an intriguing combination of blues and hillbilly boogie backed by rhythmic elements that were already used in country: the strum of the acoustic guitar, the staccato picking of the electric guitar, and the "slap" stroke of the upright bass.

When Sam Phillips began recording Carl Perkins in 1954, however, he decided to let the band include a drummer, **W.S. "Fluke" Holland**. The result - Perkins' 1956 classic "Blue Suede Shoes" - was a lethal new musical concoction, and a huge success. Backed by Holland's shuffling brushes, "Blue Suede Shoes" topped the country, pop *and* r&b charts, the first record ever to do so. It is generally acknowledged as the finest example of pure rockabilly, and forever imprinted the mark of country music on the emerging sound of rock'n'roll.

Along with Holland, another important name in rockabilly drumming is **J.M. Van Eaton**, who played on nearly two thirds of all the recordings done at Sun. Van Eaton utilized a wide variety of grooves in defining the Sun sound: a two-handed "double shuffle" on "Whole Lotta Shakin' Going On" (Jerry Lee Lewis), a heavy backbeat on "Red Hot" (Billy Lee Riley), a straight eighth pulse on "High School Confidential" (Jerry Lee Lewis), and a country-style chug on "Ballad of a Teenage Queen" (Johnny Cash).

Rock'n'Roll Crowns Its King

Although r&b and rockabilly had made significant early rumblings, it took another Sun Records star, a young Memphis truck driver named Elvis Presley, to transform rock from a number of disparate elements into a fully formed style of its own. In many ways, Elvis personified the melting pot in which rock had been brewing. He was white, bred on country, gospel and hillbilly music; but he also loved rhythm and blues, and borrowed aspects of his singing style, fashion sense and onstage persona from black entertainers he had idolized as a teenager. Elvis' good looks and polite demeanor made him rock's ultimate spokesman, particularly in the rising medium of television. Appearances on Ed Sullivan and other TV programs would turn him into a huge star, and spread the word about rock'n'roll to an international audience.

In 1955 Elvis left Sun for the major label RCA, where he was given the freedom and the backing to cobble together all his disparate influences into the ultimate prototype for fifties rock. One of his first moves was to include drummer **DJ Fontana** on all future recordings (Elvis' Sun sides had been limited to the acoustic guitar/electric guitar/upright bass instrumentation of early rockabilly). Fontana fit the eclectic bill to perfection. He was a schooled swing drummer, but had amassed a wide range of professional experience that took him from Nashville's strip clubs to the drum chair in the Louisiana Hayride house band. His energy on Elvis' RCA hits of the fifties – songs like "Jailhouse Rock," "Hound Dog" and "My Baby Left Me" – complements Presley's, and produced some of the most exciting rock drumming that had yet been committed to record.

Other Important Drummers of Early Rock

In the wake of Elvis' success, the definition of what constituted rock'n'roll widened considerably. By the end of the 1950s, the term was being applied to any number of artists with roots in country, rockabilly, rhythm and blues or pop. The unifying factor among them was almost always the heavy drive of the rhythm section. In addition to the pioneers already mentioned, several other drummers made notable contributions to the big beat of early rock:

Henry T. Green was the engine that drove The Treniers, an incredibly influential African-American proto-rock band whose career extended from 1949 well into the 1990s. With a riveting stage show and high-energy hits like "This Is It," and "Rockin' Is Our Business," the Treniers inspired countless white artists (Bill Haley in particular) to "spread the gospel" of r&b.

Dickie Harrell was the driving force behind Gene Vincent's Blue Caps. Whether setting up a slinky brush feel ("Be-Bop-a-Lula"), playing a swinging solo ("Jumps, Giggles and Shouts") or hammering it home with backbeats ("Blue Jean Bop"), Harrell's playing was the perfect compliment to Vincent's highly emotional and often savage delivery.

Jerry "J.I." Allison's innovative grooves played a big role in the sound of The Crickets, the band led by the guitarist/singer Buddy Holly. When it came to creating rhythmic textures, anything was fair game for Allison. "Peggy Sue" featured paradiddle patterns between the tom-toms, "Not Fade Away" was played on a cardboard box, and "Every Day" had Allison slapping out the groove on his pant legs!

Bobby Morris, Harvey Lang, Paul Ferrara, and **Jimmy Vincent** all contributed to the fantastic sound of ultimate showman Louie Prima. With a career tracing back to the swing era, Prima became a star reborn during the fifties. His shtick, honed in the lounges of Las Vegas, included Italian-American folk songs, swing jazz, and jump blues, all backed by a boogie-woogie style rhythm that has come to be known as "the Prima shuffle." Although Prima hits like "Just a Gigolo" and "Jump, Jive and Wail" may seem out of place in the world of early rock'n'roll, they went over big with rock audiences, and made Prima a mainstay on TV's all-powerful Ed Sullivan show.

Turn It Up! Rock Gets Its Own Instruments

In their quest to make a greater impact as both musicians and showmen, the pioneers of rock seized on the latest equipment innovations to further enhance their sound. These innovations included the electric bass and electric piano, both of which were introduced in the early fifties (amplified guitar had been a part of popular music since the 1930s). More portable than their predecessors, these instruments could better withstand changing weather conditions and other rigors of the road.

According to super-producer Quincy Jones, "[The electric bass] really changed the sound of music because it ate up so much space. Its sound was so imposing in comparison to the upright bass, so it couldn't have the same function. It allowed the rhythm section to become the stars . . . and it created a new language." (5) R&B master Ray Charles first popularized the electric piano on his 1959 crossover smash "What'd I Say." The song's funky, Latin tinged groove - played by Charles' drummer **Milt Turner** - was instrumental in paving the way for the soul music explosion of the 1960s.

For drummers, the most important equipment innovation to appear during the early rock era was the synthetic (or "plastic") drumhead. In addition to being more affordable, sonically consistent, and durable than its predecessor (the calfskin head), the plastic head could better withstand weather changes, which in the past had forced drummers to continually retune through the course of a show.

An instant sell for players, the introduction of the plastic head also had enormous implications for the drumming industry as a whole. Previously, there had been no universal standard for drum sizing, which made the marketing of drums on a global scale extremely difficult. Since plastic heads were developed and patented by only a few companies (most particularly Remo), they were limited to particular sizes. Because of the popularity of the plastic head, the world's drum companies had no choice but to match those sizes, thereby setting the universal standard that we continue to follow today.

According to Remo Belli - president of Remo, Inc. and one of several pioneers in plastic head design: "The plastic drumhead is responsible for billions of dollars worth of *business*, not in plastic drumheads but in *drum* business. It allowed the rock'n'roll phenomenon to happen, with all the touring and physical punishment on the drums that went with it. You might have had rock'n'roll [without the plastic head], but I wouldn't know how to define what it would have been like." (6)

By 1960, the innovations of rock's "big beat" – heavy backbeats and straight eighth grooves - had become the dominant force in drumming. Yet, despite the influence of rock, one could not claim that the rollicking beats behind hits like "Rock Around the Clock," "Tutti-Frutti" and "Jailhouse Rock" were played by "rock drummers." In fact, rock's architects were all reared on jazz, swing and r&b. These drummers' approach to rock'n'roll was still firmly rooted in the styles of the past, and the natural "swing" of early rock reflects that connection. Rock drumming would retain this natural sense of swing through the first two decades of its existence.

Another aspect of rock drumming notably rooted in the past was the style of playing fills. As opposed to today's fills, which incorporate long phrases covering multiple beats and ending in a cymbal crash, the earliest rock fills were short bursts that punctuated the tail end of four and eight-bar phrases. Billy Gussack's fills on "Rock Around the Clock," for example, all conclude on beat four, *not* the following beat one as is common today. His cymbal crashes (played on a *splash* cymbal) are rarely if ever accented by a bass drum stroke. In general, cymbal crashes - such a large part of the modern playing style - were rarely found in rock recordings prior to the British Invasion. Photos of the period support this claim; they reveal that most drummers of early rock did not include crash cymbals as part of their set up.

Long Live Rock! Rock is Dead?

Today, as seen through the filter of nostalgia-heavy icons like *Happy Days* and *Grease*, fifties rock'n'roll seems quaint, perhaps even a bit corny. But according to writer Robert Ventura, "There's no way to grasp the subversive force of this now-innocent-sounding music unless you can feel a little of what it meant to be a kid hearing it as it was played for the first time. The steady stream of mixed black and white rock records played on the major radio outlets began with Elvis Presley's "Heartbreak Hotel" . . . When Elvis hit the charts in 1956 there was no such thing as a "youth market." By 1957, almost solely through the demand for his recordings, there was. It was a fundamental, structural change in American society." (7)

From 1956-1958, rock'n'roll dominated the American cultural landscape. Nothing was hotter, and nothing created more of a stir. Hollywood celebrated the rock'n'roll rebel image through the likes of Marlon Brando and James Dean. Leather jackets, cuffed Levi's and ducktail haircuts dominated teen fashion, along with pedal pushers and neckerchiefs. Songs memorializing everything from unrequited love to guitars, hot rods, and other teen obsessions filled the airwaves. And once a week, a new television program called *American Bandstand* broadcast performances by the hottest acts, and relayed the latest dance crazes, from the Bop to the Hand Jive to the Stroll.

Despite all the fanfare, the coming-out party of rock'n'roll would not be an easy one. Something with so much power to affect an entire generation was also sure to be viewed as a dangerous threat. Religious and community leaders lashed out against rock'n'roll, claiming that it was leading their children into a life of juvenile delinquency. Many radio stations, vowing never to play the "devil's music," sponsored "record breakings" at which hundreds of rock discs were publicly destroyed. For some, no doubt, the fact that rock music had its roots in African-American culture was reason enough to condemn it.

Opposition was not the only hurdle facing the new music. Many of rock's earliest stars were not around long enough to enjoy the fruits of their labors. Buddy Holly, Ritchie Valens, and the Big Bopper died in a 1959 plane crash. Gene Vincent was badly injured in a car crash, which also killed his good friend Eddie Cochran. Carl Perkins' career was derailed at its peak, also by a car accident. Chuck Berry garnered a nasty reputation following several arrests, and Jerry Lee Lewis was blacklisted from radio airplay when it was discovered that he had married his thirteen-year-old cousin. After a 1959 tour of Australia, Little Richard became a "born again" Christian and left music for the ministry (at least for a few years). Bill Haley's career, already put on the skids by the much hipper Elvis, was marred by fan riots during a European tour.

The biggest rock hero of 'em all, Elvis Presley, heeded the call of Uncle Sam and was drafted into the U.S. Army in 1958. Upon returning to civilian life two years later, Elvis shifted the focus of his career to Hollywood, and the cookie-cutter B-movies he churned out during the sixties focused much more on his star status than on serious music. Presley would not perform publicly again until 1969, and by then his performances were largely Vegas-style productions, devoid for the most part of the cutting edge rock that was once his trademark.

All these distractions seriously crippled rock'n'roll at a time when it was still coming of age. The major labels, rattled by all the controversy, responded by trying to make rock'n'roll "safer." They filled the void left by Elvis and his fellow pioneers with artists who looked and sounded like rockers, but lacked the rebellious attitude and raw energy of the originals. Manufactured "teen idols" like Fabian and Bobby Rydell recorded generic sound-alike rock, while rip-off artists like Pat Boone and Georgia Gibbs cashed in on the rock phenomenon with watered down covers and novelties like "Rock'n'Roll Wedding."

In retrospect, the birth of rock'n'roll should be considered nothing short of a revolution, a unique moment in time that brought both black and white artists together under the same musical banner, and shook up society in the process. Yet, in only a few short years, that revolution had been quelled. The best elements of rock's forbearers – country blues, r&b and rockabilly - had become so digested into the common language of pop music that they no longer stood out with any impact. It would take decades before these styles would be acknowledged for their important contributions, and given a place in rock's own "Hall of Fame."

The multi-racial spirit that marked early rock had also been purged. By 1960, the rock genre was comprised of mostly white acts, and was targeted primarily to white audiences. Black music would continue to evolve on its own path, first through soul and funk, then rap and hip-hop; but to this day, black and white artists are still generally marketed to separate demographics.

The Golden Age of Rock Instrumentals

Despite the fallow period that rock'n'roll experienced in the late fifties and early sixties, the music continued to make important strides forward leading up to the monumental leap of the British Invasion. One of the brightest spots on the musical landscape during this period was the rock instrumental.

In many ways, the instrumental was a hold over from the swing era, when bandleaders and featured soloists took precedence over singers. Among the instrumental styles that wielded influence over early rock'n'roll, the most important was the sound of the so-called "honking" saxophone. Tenorman Illinois Jacquet first popularized this over-the-top approach in 1942 with his solo on Lionel Hampton's big band recording of "Flying Home." Utilizing an arsenal of squeals, grunts, growls and honks, Jacquet's soloing technique drove audiences to frenzy, and was so popular that it spawned an entire generation of players who specialized in it. By the late forties, r&b saxophonists like "Big Jay" McNeely had taken the honking style to ever more outrageous extremes, adding antics like "walking the bar," or playing the horn while lying on their backs. McNeely's uptempo romps like "3-D" and "Nervous Man, Nervous" often lasted for ten or fifteen minutes, and set the pace for the wild stage shows that are so associated with rock. McNeely's drummers, **Leonard "Tight" Hardiman** and later, **Darnell "Blimp" Cole** kept up a frenetic pace, throwing down double-time backbeats with such ferocity that this music could not be mistaken for anything except rock'n'roll.

As r&b morphed into rock, the honkin' tenor stood out as one of its biggest attractions. Players like Sam "the Man" Taylor, King Curtis and Plas Johnson immortalized the sound on countless rock'n'roll sessions, and sax favorites like "Yakety Sax" (Boots Randolph), "Harlem Nocturne" (The Viscounts) and "Night Train" (James Brown) rode the airwaves. Probably the most famous of the rock's honkin' sax instrumentals is The Champs' 1958 smash "Tequila," which features drummer **Gene Alden** playing what might be the first example of Latin rock.

Another instrument that found great success in the world of early rock'n'roll was the organ. Hammond B-3 wizard Bill Dogett broke the ice in 1956 with the r&b classic "Honky Tonk." On the strength of drummer **Shep Sheppard**'s ultra-greasy shuffle, "Honky Tonk" crossed over to the Pop charts and remained there for an amazing 22 weeks. Elvis Presley's former bass player Bill Black fronted a popular group that featured organ. Black's 1959 hit, "Smokie, Part 2," featured **Jerry Arnold** on drums. Perhaps the most famous organ instrumental of the early rock era was "Green Onions," a 1962 mega-hit for the Stax label's house band, Booker T. and the MG's. One of the first racially integrated groups to emerge in the rock era, the MG's featured the funky and musical grooves of drummer **Al Jackson, Jr.** The organ (subsequently followed by the synthesizer) would go on to help define the sound of sixties rock'n'roll, and was featured prominently in groups like the Zombies, Iron Butterfly, Deep Purple and the Doors.

The electric guitar also made great strides in the years prior to the British Invasion. In addition to Bo Diddley, a number of important innovators would totally redefine the instrument, and help it emerge as the dominant sound in rock within a few short years. Guitarist Link Wray punched holes in the speakers of his amplifier, creating a "fuzztone" effect known as distortion. Songs like "Rumble" and "Rawhide" (both featuring brother **Doug Wray** laying down a rough 12/8 feel), are arguably some of the best tracks of "real" rock to emerge in the era of the teen idol. Duane Eddy, another late fifties innovator, broadened the sound of his guitar by running it through an empty water tank used as an echo chamber. His signature "twang" opened up the low end of the instrument, and can be heard on "Rebel Rouser" and "Cannonball" (which feature the two-beat drumming of **Bob Taylor**). The Ventures, arguably the most popular instrumental rock band of all time, were one of the first to utilize the two-guitar/bass/drums lineup that would come to utterly dominate rock'n'roll in the mid-sixties. Their clean, reverb picking style (backed by drummer **Howie Johnston**) was first popularized in the 1960 smash "Walk, Don't Run," and was especially influential on the development of surf music.

Lest we not forget, rock's instrumental heyday also welcomed the return of the drum feature, relatively absent in pop music since the days of Gene Krupa and swing. In 1957, veteran swing drummer **Cozy Cole** had a surprise rock crossover smash with "Topsy, Part 2," which featured great rudimental snare drum work, thunderous tom-toms and roaring crash cymbals. Two years later, teenager **Sandy Nelson** parlayed those concepts into an entire career, releasing a slew of drum oriented instrumental rock albums like *Teen Beat* (1959) and *Let There Be Drums* (1961). In the days before Ringo Starr, Nelson was a major ambassador for the drums, and an enormous influence on a generation of young players.

With the success of Cozy Cole and Sandy Nelson, many of drumming's biggest names from a variety of genres took the opportunity to jump on the bandwagon. The late fifties and early sixties are a wonderfully rich period for drum feature records, whether from the world of swing (**Buddy Rich, Gene Krupa, Louie Bellson**), bebop (**Max Roach, Art Blakey**), or the studio (**Earl Palmer, Hal Blaine**).

In 1963, California wave rider Dick Dale blazed onto the scene. His bold guitar playing, which utilized rapid-fire picking and Middle Eastern scales, heralded the birth of a new style - surf rock. Using customized amps and a new type of solid body guitar called the Fender Stratocaster, Dale upped the volume ante, and brought the roar of the surf to life. His earliest hit "Let's Go Trippin'" featured **Drew Johnson**, while "Miserlou" highlighted the heavy pounding of West Coast studio players like **Hal Blaine**. Studio drummers were also behind the success of surf oriented vocal groups like Jan and Dean and the Beach Boys' (although their initial sessions featured **Dennis Wilson**). The Chantays (and drummer **Bob Welch**) rode the surf wave with "Pipeline." Finally, drummer **Ron Wilson** provided one of the most memorable moments of the entire surf era with his legendary breaks on The Surfaris' "Wipeout."

A popular groove that pervaded many rock recordings of this period was the so-called "surf beat," essentially a standard rock'n'roll groove that tacked on an extra snare hit to the "and" of two. The resulting kick/snare pattern ("boom, *duh-duh*, boom, *duh*") will forever be affiliated with the instrumental and surf rock of the fifties and sixties.

Early Rock'n'Roll in the Studio

As rock'n'roll became an accepted institution within the recording industry, studio drummers began to play a larger role in the creation of the music. In general, they were better schooled than the drummers who backed rock artists on the road, and with an intimate knowledge of the recording process they could work more quickly and efficiently in the pressure-filled environment of the studio.

In addition to his aforementioned work with r&b greats like Little Richard, Lloyd Price and Fats Domino, studio ace **Earl Palmer** backed many of the legends of rock. His "in the pocket" playing can be heard on hits by Eddie Cochran ("Summertime Blues"), Ritchie Valens ("C'mon, Let's Go," "La Bamba"), Ricky Nelson ("Be-Bop Baby"), Bobby Day ("Rockin' Robin), The Johnny Otis Show ("Willie and the Hand Jive"), Bobby Vee ("Devil or Angel"), Thurston Harris ("Little Bitty Pretty One"), Chan Romero ("Hippy Hippy Shake") and Sam Cooke ("You Send Me"). Palmer also released two drum feature records under his own name, *Drumsville* (1961), and *Percolator Twist* (1962).

Veteran swing drummer **Panama Francis** was a major force in the studios of New York City, backing many r&b greats, as well as scores of artists during the early years of rock'n'roll. Francis' list of recorded credits includes Screamin' Jay Hawkins ("I Put A Spell On You"), LaVern Baker ("Jim Dandy"), the Platters ("Only You," "Smoke Gets in Your Eyes,"), Jackie Wilson ("Reet Petite"), the Ravens ("Earth Angel"), Ray Charles ("Drown In My Own Tears"), Bill Haley ("Shake, Rattle and Roll"), Buddy Holly ("It Doesn't Matter Any More"), The Tokens ("The Lion Sleeps Tonight"), The Flamingoes ("I Only Have Eyes For You"), Frankie Avalon ("From Bobby Socks to Stockings"), Fabian ("Like a Tiger"), The Four Seasons ("Walk Like a Man," "Big Girls Don't Cry"), Bobby Darin ("Splish Splash"), and Neil Sedaka ("Calendar Girl"). As a studio regular, Francis was also an active participant in the invention of modern recording techniques, such as closed drum mic-ing and overdubbing.

Buddy Harman was part of Nashville's legendary "Studio Band," a crew of musicians who backed major country artists for nearly three decades. During the fifties, sixties and seventies, Harman logged over 18,000 recording sessions, and created the "one stick/one brush" shuffle that came to define the sound of country drumming. He also backed most of the early rock'n'rollers that recorded in Nashville; the list includes Johnny Burnette and The Rock'n'Roll Trio ("Rockbilly Boogie," "The Train Kept A'Rollin'"), the Everly Brothers ("Bye Bye Love," "Wake Up Little Susie"), Roy Orbison ("Oh Pretty Woman") and Johnny Cash ("Ring of Fire"). Along with **D.J. Fontana**, Harman played on the soundtrack to every one of the 33 films made by Elvis Presley during the 1960s.

Hal Blaine was perhaps drumming's first true rock'n'roll specialist, leading to his absolute domination of the session scene in Los Angeles for most of the sixties and seventies. With a willingness to explore alternative sounds, and a specialized "monster" kit that included numerous tom-toms built on prototype drum racks, Blaine became a favorite among producers and artists eager to explore the new frontier of rock. His resume reads like a "who's who" of rock history. In the sixties alone, a short list of Blaine's clients included Phil Spector's "wall of sound" sessions, Sam Cooke, The Beach Boys, The Mamas and the Papas, The Byrds, Sonny and Cher, The Monkees, The Tijuana Brass, Nancy Sinatra, The Fifth Dimension, Johnny Rivers, and Simon and Garfunkel. Blaine also released several drum feature records of his own, including *Deuces, "T's," Roadsters and Drums* (1963) and *Drums! Drums! A Go Go* (1966). Both Blaine and Earl Palmer were part of a highly influential group of L.A. musicians known as the "Wrecking Crew," which essentially crafted the blueprint for modern rock'n'roll session playing.

Other great drummers who made important studio contributions to rock'n'roll in the fifties and early sixties include: **Connie Kay**, **Calvin Sheilds**, **Joe Marshall**, **Gary Chester**, and **Jesse Sailes**.

The British Are Coming! The British Are Coming!

Going back to the earliest days of jazz and Ragtime, American pop culture had been of great fascination to the British, who perhaps because of their Victorian heritage could not themselves conceive of something so uninhibited. During WWII, when American troops brought the music and dance of swing with them to war-torn Europe, the beleaguered Brits took to it like it was their own. In the late forties, bebop had an impact that was perhaps as strong in Europe as it was in America.

Although British musicians had always done their best to play American popular music, their interpretations had for the most part come across as second-rate imitations of the real thing. In the early fifties, however, a British movement called Skiffle arose that changed everything. Skiffle was based on American blues, folk and bluegrass, and utilized the same acoustic instruments: guitars, banjos, washtub bass, and washboard. Skiffle was simple to learn and affordable enough that any youngster could pick up a guitar and start participating without too much effort. Spearheaded by Lonnie Donegan and his 1954 smash "Rock Island Line," the skiffle craze created a new guitar culture in England that would be highly influential on future trend setters like the Beatles and the Stones.

The success of skiffle was followed up the next year by rock'n'roll, and this newest American import served to energize a British youth that was struggling with the economic hardships of the post-war. Television appearances by stars like Elvis and Little Richard popularized the rock image and attitude, and in the late fifties, tours from Bill Haley and Buddy Holly influenced British movements like the Rockers and Teddy Boys. Paul McCartney has said that he and his mates in the Beatles named their band as a tribute to Buddy Holly's Crickets.

*Un*like their stateside counterparts, the British had *not* written off the American roots styles that had influenced rock'n'roll in the first place. Under the direction of Chess Records bassist/producer/impresario Willie Dixon, many great bluesman and r&b stars were "rediscovered" in Europe during the early sixties. A series of packaged tours, collectively known as the "American Folk Blues Festival," brought legendary bluesmen like Muddy Waters, Howlin' Wolf and John Lee Hooker across the Atlantic for the first time. Their concert appearances made them stars in Europe, and infatuated a new generation of British musicians, who would subsequently form groups like the Beatles, the Yardbirds, the Animals, and the Rolling Stones.

The early sixties also saw the emergence of a quality British rock'n'roll scene that had a distinct sound all its own. The most important group of this period was The Shadows, who began their career as the backing unit for Brit teen idol Cliff Richards, but split off in 1960 to become one of the most successful rock bands in British history. Often described as a British version of the Ventures, the Shadows' biggest hit was the tom-tom driven "Apache." Over a long and productive career, the Shadows featured several notable drummers, including **Tony Meehan** and **Brian Bennett**. Another British group, the Tornados, had a #1 hit in America in 1962 with the instrumental "Telstar." The group's drummer, **Clem Cattini**, would become one of the top studio drummers in England during the sixties and seventies, backing hits by Johnny Kidd and the Pirates ("Shakin' All Over,"), Joe Cocker ("With A Little Help From My Friends"), Lou Reed ("Going Down"), and the Bee Gees ("Run To Me").

Probably the *most* recorded British drummer of the early sixties, however, was **Bobby Graham**, who, alongside the likes of Jimmy Page and John Paul Jones (future founders of Led Zeppelin) and Jack Bruce (soon to be in Cream), was part of the first generation of British rock session heavyweights. Graham appeared on hits by the Kinks ("All Day and All of the Night"), Dave Berry ("The Crying Game"), the Nashville Teens ("Tobacco Road"), Brenda Lee ("Is It True"), Dusty Springfield ("I Only Want to Be With You"), and recorded with numerous other British stars like Petula Clark, Tom Jones and Rod Stewart.

Beatles, Stones and other Invaders

With all the activity on the British rock scene, it seemed only to be a matter of time before something of a much larger scope would emerge. That something arrived in 1963 in the form of a foursome out of Liverpool called The Beatles. Rock journalist Ritchie Unterberger had this to say about the profound effect that the "Fab Four" had upon rock music:

> To start with the obvious, they were the greatest and most influential act of the rock era, and introduced more innovations into popular music than any other rock band of the 20th century. Moreover, they were among the few artists of *any* discipline that were simultaneously the best at what they did *and* the most popular at what they did. Relentlessly imaginative and experimental, the Beatles grabbed a hold of the international mass consciousness in 1964 and never let go for the next six years, always staying ahead of the pack in terms of creativity but never losing their ability to communicate their increasingly sophisticated ideas to a mass audience. They established the prototype for the self-contained rock group that wrote and performed its own material. They were also unsurpassed in their eclecticism, willing to borrow from blues, popular standards, gospel, folk, or whatever seemed suitable for their musical vision. As composers, their craft and melodic inventiveness were second to none, and key to the evolution of rock from its blues/R&B-based forms into a style that was far more eclectic, but equally visceral. Their supremacy as rock icons remains unchallenged to this day, decades after their breakup in 1970. (8)

The Beatles' brand of rock'n'roll had a completely modern sound, yet it was solidly based in the genre's roots. Many of the group's early recordings are either covers of, or evoke aspects of

Elvis, Buddy Holly, Chuck Berry, Little Richard, Carl Perkins, and the Everly Brothers. The Beatles had also kept an ear open to the early sixties sounds of Motown, Phil Spector, and the girl groups. Essentially, they took the best elements of the rock and pop they loved and made them their own. Songs like "Please Please Me," "From Me to You" and "I Feel Fine," combine an unmatched songwriting savvy with infectious melodies, a brash guitar-oriented attack, and positively exuberant harmonies.

American youth, nonplussed with the lackluster rock'n'roll being released in their own country, reacted to the Fab Four as if they'd been handed the Holy Grail. The Beatles' 1964 appearances on the Ed Sullivan show were unprecedented television events that launched a craze known as "Beatlemania." Only the meteoric rise to fame of Frank Sinatra in the forties and Elvis in the fifties could compare in terms of historical significance.

Ringo Starr, the Beatles' charming and affable drummer, inspired a revolution of his own. Not since Gene Krupa thirty years earlier had any one drummer inspired so many youngsters to take up the sticks. Ringo was the leading reason that rock drummers began using the matched grip, and his signature Oyster Pearl kit was so popular that it made Ludwig the number one drum manufacturer for the next two decades. **Max Weinberg**, drummer for Bruce Springsteen's "E Street Band" and leader of the Max Weinberg Seven on *Late Night with Conan O'Brien*, eloquently described what so many drummers across the country felt:

> More than any other drummer, Ringo Starr changed my life. The impact and memory of [The Beatles] on Ed Sullivan's show will never leave me. I can still see Ringo, in the back, moving that beat with his whole body, his right hand swinging off his sock cymbal while his left hand pounds his snare. He was fantastic. I knew he was having the time of his life, and I wanted some of that. (9)

Through a simple but well-defined drumming style, Ringo gave the Beatles' music an instantly likeable bounce. His playing on classics like "Twist and Shout," "Rock and Roll Music," "She Loves You," and "I Wanna Hold Your Hand" still sounds remarkably fresh today. And his signature phrasing and staggered tom-tom fills on later Beatle tunes like "Rain," "A Day in the Life," and "Carry That Weight" rewrote the book on what was possible for a drummer to achieve in the studio.

The Beatles were the first British rock group to gain worldwide prominence, and they launched a so-called "British Invasion" that made rock'n'roll a truly international phenomenon. In the wake of The Beatles' success, a whole wave of English rock bands crossed over into the American market, where they dominated the charts from 1964 to 1966. Though not all of these bands sounded similar, each group was heavily influenced by American rock & roll, blues, and r&b.

After Ringo Starr, the most influential of the "invasion" drummers was the Rolling Stones'

Charlie Watts. Like many of the British drummers of his generation, Watts had been reared on post-war swing and bebop, which created a certain freedom and looseness to his playing. Watts also possessed a sparse feel and solid backbeat that reflected the Delta blues influence that was popular in the Stones' hometown of London. His powerful playing on "Honky Tonk Women," "Satisfaction," and "Brown Sugar" reveal a laid back power that somehow manages to remain on the edge. As a result, Watts' style remains one of the most imitated in rock.

In addition to Starr and Watts, the most influential drummers of the British Invasion included **Dave Clark**, who led his band the Dave Clark Five ("Glad All Over"), **Mick Avory** of the Kinks' ("You Really Got Me"), the Animals' **John Steel** ("We Gotta Get Out Of This Place"), **Jim McCarty** of the Yardbirds' ("For Your Love"), Manfred Mann's **Mike Hugg** ("Doo Wah Diddy"), **Bobby Elliott** of the Hollies ("Bus Stop"), and the Zombies' **Hugh Grundy** ("She's Not There").

A sub-genre of the British Invasion was the mod movement, which was defined more by its ultra-cool lifestyle and neo-Italian fashions than by a particular musical identity. British mod groups showed a heavy r&b influence, although their take on the genre was usually harder and faster than the original. The two mod bands that had success crossing over to the United States market were the Small Faces (later the Faces) with drummer **Kenny Jones**, and the Who, which featured one of the all time rock drumming legends, **Keith Moon**. Moon and the Who will be discussed at length in the next chapter.

The British Invasion also influenced the mid-sixties sound of "garage" rock, which was established primarily by American rock bands. Although less sophisticated than their British counterparts, garage bands infused their music with a rawness reminiscent of the earliest days of rock'n'roll. The granddaddy of the garage bands is most likely the Seattle band the Wailers (featuring drummer **Mike Burk**), who were still teenagers when their raunchy 1959 hit "Tall Cool One" hit the American charts. In the mid-sixties, garage favorites like The Kingsmen ("Louie Louie," **Lyn Easton**), the Seeds ("Pushin' Too Hard," **Rick Andridge**), Paul Revere and the Raiders ("Steppin' Out," **Mike Smith**) and the Bobby Fuller Four ("I Fought the Law," **James Reece**) brought the movement into the mainstream. And the Rascals ("Good Lovin,'" "Groovin," **Dino Danelli**), wed the garage concept with the popular black music of the day, creating a movement known as "blue eyed soul."

Chapter Two: The Sixties

By the middle of the 1960's, rock'n'roll drumming had settled on a stable, recognizable formula, and although it has since been expressed in a million-and-one variations, that formula remains intact to the present day. Post-Invasion rock drumming was now heavily dominated by straight eighth grooves, and as opposed to the lighter, cymbal oriented shuffles which had characterized early rock, mid-sixties drummers relied more and more on heavy kick and snare combinations to drive the band. Whereas drum fills in the 1950s had mimicked those from the swing era, rock fills of the sixties were played across multiple tom-toms, and nearly always concluded with a cymbal crash on the following beat one (accentuated by a bass drum stroke).

More and more, drummers were freely switching between hi hat and ride cymbal in their time keeping, another departure from early rock, in which they tended to stick to one element or the other. And late sixties rock would see an explosion in double bass drum set ups, first introduced and popularized by **Louie Bellson** and other swing era drummers nearly three decades earlier. To keep up with the ever-increasing volume of electronic instruments, P.A. systems, and venue sizes, drummers continued to play harder and louder with each passing year.

As if to answer the critics of the previous decade, the expression "rock'n'roll is here to stay" became a popular slogan in the 1960s. In fact, rock'n'roll was now the dominant force in pop music, and all the essential elements were in place that would carry it through to the end of the twentieth century. As a result, further discussions of rock'n'roll in this book will shift from the elements that gave birth to the music, to the various sub-genres and hybrid styles that have defined rock'n'roll since the mid-sixties.

Rock'n'Roll as Art and Lifestyle

With the British Invasion serving as its impetus, the remainder of the 1960s spawned a growth period in rock'n'roll that is perhaps unequalled in the music's history. The rise of the Civil Rights Movement and the escalation of the Vietnam War had dramatic effects upon American society, causing enormous upheavals to the cultural and moral fabric of the nation. Young people began to systematically question the values and motives of the institutions around them, and started exploring nonconformist lifestyles as a means of changing those institutions. As the voice of this so-called "counterculture," rock music took on heavy left-wing political overtones. It also began to reflect the growing popularity of drug use and "free love" that were hallmarks of the "hippie" lifestyle.

With a decade of music making under their collective belts, rock musicians were becoming better skilled at their craft, and more sophisticated in their approach. Advances in recording technology allowed rock artists to create more elaborate arrangements, and many began dropping the traditional three-minute pop format altogether in favor of longer, more complex compositions. By the end of the decade, extended instrumental explorations and improvisational jams became standard rock fare. Many artists also started blending rock with other musical styles, such as jazz and classical, as well as with the rhythms and instrumentation of non-

Western cultures. Others focused on deconstructing the music, taking it in experimental or avant-garde directions, and emphasizing sonic textures as opposed to conventional melodies and lyrics.

By the decade's end, rock'n'roll would become accepted as a viable art form, complete with its own journals (*Rolling Stone*, *Creem*), its own critics (Lester Bangs, Robert Christgau) and its own socio-political statements (such as Woodstock), which would serve as linchpins to define an era.

One of the musical styles that blended well with rock was folk music, a populist expression that had been around since the days of the Depression. In the early 1960s, Bob Dylan spearheaded an American folk resurgence that was quite popular on college campuses and established him as the unofficial "poet laureate" of his generation. In 1965, Dylan supplemented his acoustic sound with a full band, creating in the process what would come to be known as "folk rock." His band, a unit that once backed Arkansas rockabilly singer Ronnie Hawkins, included drummer **Levon Helm**. They brought a stripped down, rootsy sound to Dylan classics like "Maggie's Farm," and "Like A Rolling Stone," and would go on to release highly acclaimed albums (like 1968's *Songs From the Big Pink*) under their own moniker, The Band. In following Dylan's lead, both the Byrds ("Mister Tambourine Man," **Michael Clark**) and Buffalo Springfield ("For What It's Worth," **Dewey Martin**) successfully integrated the acoustic sound of folk (especially the 12-string guitar) into the rock of the British Invasion. Folk rock would grow to include elements of country (check out Bob Dylan's 1969 work *Nashville Skyline*, **Kenny Buttrey**), and eventually evolved into what became known as "the West Coast sound" in the 1970s.

Psychedelic Rock

As drugs became more popular within the counterculture as a means of reaching higher realms of consciousness, they showed an increased influence on rock music as well. More and more, rock'n'rollers created their music while on drugs, often with the express intention that listeners should experience it while in a similar state. In 1967, the Beatles officially ushered in the "psychedelic era" with *Sgt. Pepper's Lonely Hearts Club Band*, which included "Lucy in the Sky With Diamonds," an ode to the hallucinogen LSD. As landmark a recording as rock would ever see, *Sgt. Pepper* used wildly disparate instrumentation through its 13 tracks (including brass band, string orchestra, harpsichord, Mellotron, Hammond organ, sitar, tamboura and bongo drums!), seamlessly blending them all into what is widely considered the first rock'n'roll "concept" album. *Sgt. Pepper* was also a landmark in rock'n'roll production, building upon the backward tape loops and other sound effects that the Beatles had begun using on their previous release, *Revolver*. Essentially, *Sgt. Pepper* broke all the rules to a thrilling effect, and its release opened the door for rock bands to try literally anything (for better or worse).

The best psychedelic rock coupled fuzz guitars, sitars, exotic keyboards, heavy reverb, and numerous electronic effects with long improvisational jams to create a hypnotic, trance-inducing effect. Obviously, drums could be used to great effect in that capacity. **Charlie Watts'** relentless tom-tom groove gave The Rolling Stones' "Paint it Black" an edge of menace, while **Nick Mason** drove Pink Floyd's twelve-minute opus "A Saucerful of Secrets" with a seemingly endless flow of sixteenth notes. The Jefferson Airplane's "White Rabbit" is backed by the melancholic funeral march of **Spencer Dryden,** while **Preston Ritter**'s reverb drenched rimshots sound like gun blasts on the Electric Prunes' "I Had Too Much to Dream Last Night."

One of the more inventive drummers of the psychedelic era was the Doors' **John Densmore**. On his band's self-titled debut album, Densmore delivered a whole host of rhythms, from Latin beats ("Break on Through," "Light My Fire") and jazz-inflected raga ("The End"), to funky blues ("Back Door Man") and driving rock ("Take It Easy"). Perhaps the ultimate exercise in psychedelic drumming was undertaken by **Ron Bushy** in Iron Butterfly's magnum opus "In-A-Gadda-Da-Vida." Though nearly half of the seventeen-minute song was taken up by an extended drum solo, "In-A-Gadda-Da-Vida" still managed to garner extensive radio airplay, and spent a year in the top ten. Other important psychedelic groups included Love ("Seven and Seven Is," **Alban Pfisterer**), Procol Harum ("A Whiter Shade of Pale," **Bobby Harrison**), Donovan ("Sunshine Superman," **Bobby Orr**), and the Beach Boys ("Wouldn't It Be Nice," **Hal Blaine**).

Known for its ideals of peace, love and "flower power," San Francisco became the ultimate hippie mecca, and emerged as the capitol of the American psychedelic scene in 1966. For such a small city, the City by the Bay produced an exceptional number of great rock bands, which were in turn supported by equally exceptional venues like the Fillmore and the Avalon Ballroom. In addition to the Jefferson Airplane, the Bay Area was home to Country Joe and the Fish ("I-Feel-Like-I'm-Fixin'-to-Die Rag," **Chicken Hirsh**), Moby Grape ("Omaha," **Don Stevenson**), Big Brother and the Holding Company ("Piece of My Heart," **David Getz**), and Blue Cheer ("Summertime Blues," **Paul Whaley**).

San Francisco was also the birthplace of the Grateful Dead, the psychedelic era's most beloved musical ambassadors and its most enduring survivors. Although they had a few radio hits like "Truckin'" and "Uncle John's Band," the Dead were best known for their marathon live shows. Supported by a cult following known as the "Deadheads," the group remained one of the world's top grossing touring acts into the early 1990s. The Dead were the first of a number of important rock bands to popularize a two-drummer line up, comprised of **Bill Kreutzman** (who brought a lighter, jazzy style) and **Mickey Hart,** (who would go on to become a major proponent of world rhythms and percussion with his group Planet Drum). From the seventies onward, most Dead shows included a free form interlude known as "DrumSpace," in which the two drummers would improvise together using an enormous collection of drums and percussion collectively known as "the Beast."

As opposed to most of the well known 1960s Bay Area rock bands, Creedence Clearwater

25

Revival shied away from the indulgences of psychadelia, preferring an economic synthesis of rockabilly, swamp pop, r&b, and country that produced a cavalcade of top ten hits between 1969 and 1972. **Doug Clifford**'s chunky, loping beats drove classic Creedence favorites like "Bad Moon Rising," Down On the Corner" and "Fortunate Son," which managed to evoke enduring images of Americana and reflect burning social issues of the day.

Northern California was also the home of what might be considered "multicultural rock." In the late sixties, a number of bands, most particularly Santana ("Black Magic Woman," **Michael Shrieve**, later **Graham Lear**), Sly and the Family Stone ("Dance To the Music," **Greg Errico**, later **Andy Newmark**), and Tower of Power ("What Is Hip?" **David Garibaldi**) each developed a unique style based on the fusion of rock'n'roll with latin, soul, and/or funk rhythms. In keeping with the "one world" idealism of the times, these bands all featured mixed race lineups, and their material tended to reflect the positive outlook so prevalent in the sixties.

Proto-Punk and Art Rock

Psychedelic rock was tempered by the more down to earth grittiness of proto-punk, which is often sited as having its birthplace in Detroit. As opposed to the lofty and Utopian aims of the psychedelic bands, this group of mid-sixties rockers attacked the music with a simple, hard-driving energy. Their viewpoint exposed the dark underbelly of rock, and their approach valued attitude over polish. The movement had its beginnings with Detroit garage bands like the Amboy Dukes ("Journey to the Center of the Mind," **Dave Palmer**) and ? and the Mysterions ("96 Tears," **Eddie Serrato**), as well as hard-rocking blue-eyed soul bands like Mitch Ryder & the Detroit Wheels ("Devil With A Blue Dress," **Johnny "Bee" Badanjek**), which were influenced by R&B and early rock & roll.

The Detroit scene really hit its stride in the late sixties, with the emergence of MC-5 ("Kick Out the Jams," **Dennis Thompson**) and Iggy Pop and The Stooges ("Search and Destroy," **Scott Asheton**). Their aggressive approach, intense political stance and extreme stage shows had an enormous influence on the punk rock movement that would emerge in the following decade. The no-nonsense temperament of the Detroit scene also played a significant role in the development of American hard rock in the 1970s. Grand Funk Railroad ("I'm Your Captain," **Don Brewer**), Ted Nugent (Stranglehold," **Cliff Davies**), and Bob Seger ("Travelin' Man," **Charlie Allan Smith**) all emerged out of the hard charging "Motor City" to achieve widespread acclaim.

In New York City, a variety of bands - notably the Velvet Underground - were pursuing a more artistic and experimental vision of rock. Although they never achieved mainstream success, the Velvets are considered to be among the most influential bands in rock history. **Maureen Tucker**, one of the genre's important female drummers, kept the Velvets' music rooted in traditional rock rhythms ("Waiting For My Man," "White Light, White Heat"), while the bands' other members overlaid abstract (and often disturbing) lyrical images, feedback and other sound textures. With their manager, the *avant garde* artist Andy Warhol, the Velvet Undergound also set about dissecting the classic macho rock image, exploring androgyny and other "gender-bending" ideas that would soon become commonplace among rock acts ranging from David Bowie to the New York Dolls.

Frank Zappa treated *his* rock group as an orchestra, using ever-changing lineups as a canvas on which to paint his eclectic and wildly unconventional rock'n'roll vision. A student of twentieth century classical composers like Edgar Varese, Zappa drew his influences from seemingly every corner of the musical realm, fearlessly blending rock'n'roll conventions with doo-wop and r&b, jazz, reggae, avant-garde classical, even opera. Generally, Zappa's lyrics were satiric in nature - slamming everything from corporations to wannabe gurus – but his extreme use of odd time signatures, perilous harmonic runs and complex rhythmic groupings made his music some the most challenging in all of rock.

Zappa's first group, The Mother's of Invention, included drummers **Jim Black** and **Billy Mundi**. However, beginning in the late sixties, Zappa consistently employed many of the world's elite studio and journeyman players, among them **Aynsley Dunbar, Jim Gordon, John Guerin, Ralph Humphrey, Chester Thompson, Terry Bozzio, Vinnie Colaiuta** and **Chad Wackerman**. Zappa and experimental artists like Brian Eno and Kraftwerk were some of the first rockers to make use of synthesizers (a 1950s invention), as well as early versions of drum machines. Other rock artists in the "art" or "experimental" category include Captain Beefheart (**John "Drumbo" French**), Can (**Jaki Leibezeit**), Pere Ubu (**Scott Krauss**), and later Talking Heads (**Chris Frantz**) and Sonic Youth (**Steve Shelley**).

Heavy Metal: Rock's Harder Sounds

Although rock'n'roll had become increasingly amplified since its inception in the fifties, the genre would reach new heights of volume and intensity with the arrival of heavy metal (also known as "hard rock," "acid rock" or simply "metal").

According to the All Music Guide: "Of all rock & roll's myriad forms, heavy metal is the most extreme in terms of volume, machismo, and theatricality. There are numerous stylistic variations on heavy metal's core sound, but they're all tied together by a reliance on loud, distorted guitars (usually playing repeated riffs) and simple, pounding rhythms. Heavy metal has become one of the most consistently popular forms of rock music ever created, able to adapt to the times yet keep its core appeal intact." (10)

The first seeds of heavy metal were sown in the British blues scene of the early sixties. Inspired by the American masters of acoustic blues, many Englishmen began to play the music, most importantly Alexis Corner with his group Blues Incorporated (**Charlie Watts**, later **Graham Burbridge** and **Ginger Baker**), and John Mayall's Bluesbreakers (**Aynsley Dunbar**, later **Mick Fleetwood**). These artists spearheaded an early sixties London blues scene that first introduced the music to future British Invaders like the Rolling Stones and the Yardbirds. By 1966, a new generation of British bluesmen like Fleetwood Mac ("Oh Well," **Mick Fleetwood**), Ten Years After (I'm Going Home," **Ric Lee**) and Savoy Brown ("Train to Nowhere," **Roger Earl**) were squaring off the shuffle pattern of the blues, giving it a heavier feel by emphasizing the drive of the kick and snare. Energized by psychedelic and garage rock, these bands utilized the distorted sound of amplified guitars and bass to create their own interpretation of the blues.

By the end of the decade, this overdriven style of blues-rock hit its stride via the explosive sound (and popularity) of bands like the Who, the Jimi Hendrix Experience, Cream, Led Zeppelin, Black Sabbath and Deep Purple. Having been raised in the post-war environment of 1950s England, the drummers that played in these bands shared several defining traits. All were reared on American swing, r&b and bebop jazz, listing drummers like Gene Krupa, Buddy Rich, Earl Palmer and Max Roach as influences. Because of that connection to rock's roots, each had a keen awareness of the swung 8th note, a strong sense of improvisation, and highly developed hand/foot technique. Nurtured by the wide-open environment of the 1960s music business, each developed a distinct personality as a player, and was able to make a strong contribution to the character of his band. Collectively, they would have an enormous and unprecedented influence on rock drumming that continues unabated to this day.

The Who's **Keith Moon** was a wildly exhibitionist character, whose impulsive lifestyle and heavy alcohol and drug use resonated in a playing style that seemed to be equally out of control. Yet, there was a method to Moon's madness, and though it often appeared that he spent more time playing fills than grooves, his drumming provided the perfect complement to the Who's titanic sound. Moon's power was already apparent in the band's earliest mod-inflected hits ("Can't Explain," "Pictures of Lilly," and "My Generation"), and his bashing grooves and bombastic fills lent a sense of orchestral drama to the bands' groundbreaking rock operas: *Tommy* and *Quadrophenia*. In the seventies, Moon's style matured to a degree, and classic rock staples like "Baba O'Reilly," "Won't Get Fooled Again" and "Who Are You" reveal drum parts that fit beautifully into the overall song structure. Sadly, Moon's excessive lifestyle caught up with him in 1978, when he was found dead at only 31 years of age.

By the time he helped form the blues-rock power trio Cream in 1966, **Ginger Baker** was already a well-known jazz and blues player on the London scene. Cream, which also featured guitar ace Eric Clapton and bassist/vocalist Jack Bruce, was renowned for a rare ability to take songs and arrange them into acts of spontaneous beauty onstage. The band covered a lot of musical ground in its relatively short career, with songs ranging from traditional blues ("Crossroads") to hard rock ("White Room"), psychedelic jazz-rock ("Tales of Brave Ulysses") and latin-inflected pop ("I Feel Free"). Baker's idiosyncratic presence is stamped all over Cream's sound, from his "backwards beat" in "Sunshine of Your Love" (the kick and snare are reversed), to the heavy double bass work that drove the drum feature "Toad." By the time of Cream's demise, Baker was a superstar in his own right, particularly among drummers who worshipped his Krupa-like power and charisma. He went on to a successful solo career, both with supergroups like Blind Faith, and his own Ginger Baker's Air Force.

Mitch Mitchell was a versatile wizard whose prodigious drumming with the Jimi Hendrix Experience vaulted that group to the greatest heights of rock legendry. Mitchell was not a mere sideman to Hendrix, but an important collaborator. Always changing rhythms, never predictable, his playing responded perpetually to Hendrix's vibrant guitar lines. Mitchell's thrilling drum parts on "Fire," "Manic Depression," "Third Stone From the Sun" and "Little Wing" reveal a technique based in the polyrhythms of jazz as much as in rock, and his live explorations with the guitarist are some of the best of the period. In 1969-70, Hendrix collaborated with noted blues/soul drummer **Buddy Miles** (formerly of the Electric Flag), who lent his authentic shuffle to "Rainy Day, Dream Away" on the psychedelic masterpiece *Electric Ladyland*, and grooved hard with Hendrix's post-Experience group, the Band of Gypsys ("Machine Gun," "Them Changes").

Less subtle, but no less influential was **Bill Ward**, whose group Black Sabbath was the first to bring a dark mysticism to rock'n'roll. Sabbath's murky, leaden guitar riffs created doomed fantasy worlds, and brought singer Ozzy Osbourne's lyrical visions of drugs and the occult to life. Ward's drumming on "War Pigs," "Paranoid," "Iron Man" and "Sweet Leaf" reveals fearsome technique and inspired fills, but also a series of clever, thought-out groove patterns that would set the tone for generations of future "Metal Avengers," from Iron Maiden to Metallica.

Although consistently under-appreciated for his contributions, Deep Purple's **Ian Paice** was another highly influential drummer to emerge out of the British hard rock scene. One of rock's best-known left handed drummers, Paice's free-wheeling style, solid power, and breathtaking speed fueled Deep Purple's distortion-driven brand of blues-rock. His unrelenting intensity blended well with the catchy guitar riffs, soaring vocals and warm Hammond organ pads that produced rock anthems like "Hush," "Highway Star," "Woman From Tokyo," and especially "Smoke on the Water." Paice's playing is particularly strong on "Fireball," (note the impressive double bass intro) and on his drum feature, "The Mule."

Of all the British groups to emerge out of the sixties blues-rock scene, the one that can make the superlative claim to the title "first heavy metal band" is Led Zeppelin. From its inception in 1968, Zeppelin played blues tunes heavier and louder than anyone before it, and by the early seventies, the band had created its own epic, textured brand of heavy rock. With the possible exception of Ringo Starr, Zeppelin's **John Bonham** left a stamp on the sound and feel of rock drumming that redefined the genre like no other. Bonham's tremendous power and oversized drums produced booming bass drum thuds, chunky backbeats and bottomless cymbal crashes that gave songs like "When the Levee Breaks" and "Kashmir" an instantly identifiable quality, and set a standard for rock drum production that still stands today.

Beyond his sound, Bonham's riveting playing is the primary reason for his legacy's continuing dominance. Simply put, Bonham took rock drumming to a new level. He handled Zeppelin's many musical references with ease, coloring his distinctive style with rollicking triplets ("Good Times, Bad Times"), slow 12/8 grinds ("Since I've Been Loving You"), hard-driving straight eighths ("Rock'n'Roll"), odd-metered stumbles ("The Crunge"), half-time funk shuffles ("Fool in the Rain") and brute simplicity ("Stairway to Heaven"). Bonham's signature solo feature, "Moby Dick," found him playing with his hands, and hammering on tympani and gongs, all accompanied by the steady eighth-note "chick" of a tambourine mounted to his hi-hat. One can only imagine Bonham's further contribution to rock drumming had his life not been tragically cut short in 1980.

By the end of the sixties, scores of bands had emerged in the vein of the British hard rock acts. Although many of these bands relied on image and attitude as selling points, several made noteworthy musical contributions. Vanilla Fudge ("You Keep Me Hangin' On") featured **Carmine Appice**, one of the more dominant drummers of early metal whose later accomplishments included work with Jeff Beck, Rod Stewart and Ted Nugent. Appice, whose extreme power and double bass work made him highly influential, is also the author of *Realistic Rock*, one of the most popular and enduring drum instructional books of all time.

The American group Steppenwolf (with drummer **Jerry Edmonton**) hit big in 1968 with "Born To Be Wild," which became an instant rock classic when it was featured in the hippie biker epic *Easy Rider*. The song's reference to "heavy metal thunder" became the source for the emerging genre's name. Other quality heavy rock acts of the period included Free ("Alright Now," **Simon Kirke**), the James Gang ("Walk Away," **Jim Fox**), Uriah Heep ("Easy Livin'," **Lee Kerslake**), Nazareth ("Hair of the Dog," **Darrell Sweet**), and Thin Lizzy ("The Boys Are Back in Town," **Brian Downey**).

Progressive Rock: Pushing the Envelope

As heavy metal sought out new extremes in volume, progressive rock (a.k.a. "prog-rock") evolved as an attempt to elevate rock music to new levels of artistic credibility. The mostly British phenomenon suggested that rock was more than just teenagers' music and should be taken seriously as an art form. Prog-rock emerged out of the British psychedelic scene in 1967, specifically via a strain of classical/symphonic rock led by groups like the Nice ("America," **Brian Davison**) and the Moody Blues ("Knights in White Satin," **Graeme Edge**). The concept was firmly established with the 1969 debut of King Crimson ("21st Century Schizoid Man," **Michael Giles,** later **Ian Wallace**, then **Bill Bruford**), a band that utilized elements like the

Mellotron (a "programmable" analog keyboard), surreal guitar effects from leader Robert Fripp, and unusual melodies that often resembled Gregorian chants.

Freer in form than classical music, but not as improvisational as jazz, prog-rock employed multi-sectioned pieces that often involved elaborate arrangements and multiple time signatures. It was not uncommon for a single prog tune to the last the full side of an album. This often led critics to malign the movement as pretentious and self-indulgent, but it did not stop a variety of prog bands from achieving significant mainstream success throughout the seventies. Leading the pack was Yes, which featured drummer **Bill Bruford**, and later **Alan White**. Bruford's signature high-pitched snare drum and jazzy hand technique brought a looseness and elasticity to Yes' early successes like "Roundabout," "Starship Trooper," and "Close To the Edge," while Alan White's straight forward rock approach suited the band's sound on later hits like "Going For the One" and lengthy album cuts like "The Gates of Delirium."

Although he left Yes in 1972, Bruford continued to be highly influential in defining the progressive genre. He did a very brief stint as a second drummer in Genesis, and then joined prog-mavericks King Crimson in the mid-seventies for albums like *Lark's Tongues in Aspic* and *Red*. In 1977, he formed the band UK with guitarist Allan Holdsworth, and fronted his own self-titled solo band, both of which melded the prog concept with elements of jazz and fusion music. In 1981, he rejoined King Crimson for the highly influential *Discipline* era. During this period, Bruford was one of the first drummers to experiment extensively with electronic Simmons drums, and his hybrid kits (combining electric, acoustic and percussive elements) foreshadowed an electronic explosion that would dominate the sound of eighties rock.

Like Yes, the English band Genesis took a highly theatrical approach to rock and roll, turning its shows into costumed spectacles, and creating albums that soared with symphonic ambition. **Phil Collins** - prior to his second career as a pop superstar - approached the drum chair in Genesis as if he were kicking a big band. Collins displayed ample melodic figures and dazzling odd-time work on album cuts like "Watcher of the Skies," and "Supper's Ready." Upon the departure of singer Peter Gabriel in 1976, Collins came out front to take on lead vocal duties, adding **Chester Thompson** as a touring drummer. Thereafter, Genesis concerts always included intricate drum duets, often as part of the epic work, "The Cage." Collins continued to play drums on Genesis' studio albums, and as the band's sound turned more commercial, songs like "Turn It On Again" established the tom-tom driven signature sound that would underscore Collins' enormously successful solo career ("In the Air Tonight").

Nick Mason provided a simpler, more deliberate rhythmic feel in his drumming with the British prog/art group Pink Floyd. Although Floyd's roots were in the British psychedelic movement, by the early 1970s the band was releasing albums more conceptual in theme, produced – particularly in the case of *Dark Side of the Moon* - with an intricacy that set the standard for rock's next decade. *Dark Side*, which remained on the Billboard Album Chart for an astonishing

741 weeks, featured an innovative use of roto-toms ("Time"), searing gospel vocals ("The Great Gig in the Sky"), and probably the first top forty hit written in 7/4 time ("Money").

The heyday of progressive rock produced a whole host of successful bands. Jethro Tull ("Aqua Lung," **Clive Bunker**) and Traffic ("Mr. Fantasy," **Jim Capaldi**) both utilized acoustic instruments and Elizabethan imagery, while Emerson, Lake and Palmer ("Karn Evil Nine," **Carl Palmer**) relied heavily on the sound of keyboards. Kansas ("Point of Know Return," **Phil Ehart**) offered a radio friendly version of progressive rock, while Gentle Giant ("Free Hand," **Martin Smith**, later **Malcolm Mortimer**) took the genre into some of its most avant-garde and esoteric directions.

Jazz Rock and Fusion

Another important musical hybrid created in the late sixties was fusion, which mixed improvisational elements of jazz with the power and rhythms of rock. According to the All Music Guide, "Up until around 1967, the worlds of jazz and rock were nearly completely separate. But as rock became more creative and its musicianship improved, and as some in the jazz world became bored with hard bop and shied away from avant-garde music, the two different idioms began to trade ideas and occasionally combine forces." (11)

The birth of fusion is often credited to trumpeter Miles Davis, whose late sixties albums *In a Silent Way* (**Tony Williams**) and *Bitches Brew* (**Lenny White** and **Jack DeJohnette**, with percussionist **Don Alias**) tossed electric instruments and rock/funk beats into the jazz arena. These landmark jazz-rock recordings became popular with hippie audiences, and helped Davis emerge as a mainstream artist, performing on rock bills for audiences who knew very little about jazz. Davis dedicated the remainder of his career to the blending of multiple musical styles, and the musicians he employed on the *Bitches Brew* sessions all graduated to create the framework for what is considered fusion (also referred to as "jazz-fusion," or "rock-fusion").

Weather Report was formed by two of these alumni, keyboardist Joe Zawinul and saxophonist Wayne Shorter. This jazz-rock "supergroup," which incorporated a revolving roster of luminaries (like virtuoso electric bassist Jaco Pastorius), would remain on the cutting edge of the genre for most of its fifteen-year career. Along the way, Weather Report roped in some of the world's top drummers, taking advantage of each player's individual strengths to augment the band's ever changing amalgam of jazz, rock, funk, Latin and other ethnic musics. Among those contributions were the soulful feel of **Alphonse Mouzon** (*Weather Report*), the straight ahead style of **Eric Gravatt** (*Sweetnighter*), the hard swing of **Peter Erskine** (*Mr. Gone*), the Latin influence of **Alex Acuña** (*Heavy Weather*), and the contemporary funk-r&b of **Chester Thompson** (*Black Market*) and **Omar Hakim** (*Record*).

John McLaughlin, the guitarist on *Bitches Brew*, was allied with any number of fusion projects throughout the seventies. The most important of these was the Mahavishnu Orchestra, which featured **Billy Cobham**, another Miles Davis alum who is commonly considered the greatest practitioner of the fusion style. Cobham's tremendous strength and phenomenal dexterity powered albums like *The Inner Mounting Flame* and *Birds of Fire*, and inspired a whole new school of drumming that would produce contemporary giants like **Dennis Chambers** and **Vinnie Colaiuta**. In 1973, Cobham left Mahavishnu to chart fusion's course with his own influential group, Spectrum (*Spectrum*). Frequent collaborations with like-minded players such as guitarist John Scofield and keyboardist George Duke have kept Cobham in the spotlight for decades, and produced a body of work that defines adventurous drumming at its best.

Cobham's replacement in Mahavishnu was the 21-year old **"Narada" Michael Walden**, a *wunderkind* whose talents lay not only behind a kit, but as a composer, singer and producer as well. Although his stellar performance on 1974's *Apocalypse* was a major milestone in fusion drumming, it quickly became clear that Walden's tastes ran in a variety of musical directions. In addition to recording albums with established artists like Jeff Beck (*Wired*) and Chick Corea (*My Spanish Heart*), Walden released a string of solo albums on which he played drums and keyboards, sang, and explored a new production concept known as programming. His abilities in this arena allowed Walden to emerge as a top-notch producer in the eighties, where he found great success with projects like the multi-platinum, Grammy-winning soundtrack to *The Bodyguard*.

The seminal fusion band Return to Forever was formed by keyboardist Chick Corea, another Miles Davis prodigy from *Bitches Brew*. With its self-titled debut and *Light As a Feather* (both of which featured Brazilian drummer/percussionist **Airto Moreira**), RTF's early music incorporated a lighter, Latin-tinged style. When Corea brought on guitarist Al Dimeola and jazz-rock drummer **Lenny White**, however, the band took on a synth-heavy rock sound akin to many progressive rock bands of the day, leading to breakthrough commercial success with the Top 40 releases *Where Have I Known You Before* and *Romantic Warrior*. With his acclaimed Elektric band (featuring the staggering drumming of **Dave Weckl**), Corea would continue to carry the torch of fusion into the 21st century.

Any discussion of fusion can not overlook **Tony Williams**, a towering figure who redefined the face of both straight ahead and avant-garde jazz in his stint in Miles Davis' band from 1963-69. Always known as a hard-hitting drummer, Williams was also a dedicated fan of rock music, and upon leaving Davis he formed the seminal fusion trio Lifetime (*Emergency!*) with organist Larry Young and guitarist John McLaughlin (later Allan Holdsworth). Williams would bounce back and forth between jazz and rock influenced projects for the remainder of his career. Although he seldom strayed from his jazz roots, drummer **Jack DeJohnette** also made important contributions to the world of fusion, particularly in the form of his own ensembles, Directions (*New Rags*) and Special Edition (*Special Edition*).

Other notable entries that came to the fusion arena from jazz, rock and funk include Jean Luc-Ponty (**Casey Scheurell, Steve Smith**, and **Rayford Griffin**), Jeff Beck (**Aynsley Dunbar, Cozy Powell, Ed Greene, Richard Bailey** and **Simon Phillips**), Don Ellis (**Ralph Humphrey, Ronnie Dunn, Dave Crigger**), Al DiMeola (**Lenny White, Steve Gadd**), Herbie Hancock's Head Hunters (**Bill Summers**) and Mwandishi (**Billy Hart, Leon "Ndugu" Chancellor**), the Brecker Brothers (**Harvey Mason, Chris Parker**), Steps Ahead, (**Steve Gadd, Peter Erskine, Steve Smith**), Stanley Clarke (**Gerry Brown, Billy Cobham**), George Duke (**Leon "Ndugu" Chancellor)**, the Crusaders (**Stix Hooper**), and Tom Scott's L.A. Express (**John Guerin**).

Glam: Redefining Rock's Image

Since the earliest days of rock'n'roll, image had always played an integral role in the music's sales pitch. The sixties, with its "anything goes" attitude, had exploded that image into a colorful pastiche of costumes and outfits that ranged from Chelsea boots to Nehru jackets to the leather-clad biker look reminiscent of rock's beginnings. By the end of the decade, rockers began crossing the "ultimate" image barrier - the one that separated genders. Long hair had been part of the male rock image since the mid-sixties, but the early seventies brought far greater experimentation with makeup, androgynous clothing and sexual preference. An increasing number of male vocalists also began singing in a high-pitched or falsetto range, one that was traditionally associated with females.

Despite the homosexual inferences, these gender-bending experiments were intended to create an explicitly masculine effect, and by the early seventies they culminated in a (primarily British) movement known as glam rock. For glam bands, style *was* the statement, and with a heavy emphasis on camp, attitude and overt sexuality, glam rockers contributed some of the genre's most enduring image concepts. Countless rock bands began wearing makeup and androgynous outfits, with future monsters of rock like KISS and Mötley Crüe eventually taking the glam look to absolute extremes. Although the focus was on image, the glam movement also added a great many trashy, bubble gum anthems to the rock repertoire, notably "Bang a Gong," (T-Rex, **Bill Legend**), "All The Young Dudes" (Mott the Hoople, **Dale "Buffin" Griffen**), "Rock and Roll, Pt. 1&2" (Gary Glitter, **Mike Leander, Peter Phipps**), "Cum On Feel the Noize," (Slade, **Don Powell**), and "Fox on the Run," (Sweet, **Mick Tucker**).

Glam rock also had its artistic innovators, most particularly the theatrical persona of David Bowie ("Ziggy Stardust," **Mick "Woody" Woodmansey**). Along with bands like Roxy Music ("Love is the Drug," **Paul Thompson**) and Japan ("Suburban Love," **Steve Jansen**), Bowie's vision of glam was more dramatic and ambitious, both in terms of sound and lyrical content. His long and influential career as a rock icon had its first commercial successes with the glam-inspired characters of Ziggy Stardust and Aladdin Sane. The only American glam band of note was the New York Dolls ("Personality Crisis," **Jerry Nolan**), who coupled a shambling, cross-dressed appearance with a gritty Stones-flavored sound. Although they never came close to achieving commercial success, the Dolls (along with sixties proto-punkers like Iggy Pop's Stooges) would have a major impact on New York's emerging punk rock scene.

Chapter Three: The Seventies

By the 1970s, rock'n'roll music had become an accepted part of mainstream Western culture, and as the musical focal point of the baby boom generation, was a billion dollar industry. The rock explosion was supported by FM radio, which had grown in popularity since making the switch to stereo broadcasting in the 1960s. With a higher quality sound, FM stations became the new frontier in rock, often adopting a "free form" approach and playing album cuts considered too lengthy or esoteric for the more pop-oriented AM dial. The album format had taken over almost exclusively from the single as the vehicle for presenting rock music, and as the decade wore on, artists devised ever more creative album packaging as a means to bring their music to life.

Rock as Spectacle

With the ongoing successes of groups like the Rolling Stones, Led Zeppelin and the Who, rock concerts were now regularly taking place in sporting arenas and stadiums. Larger than life effects such as mechanized stages, laser light shows, exploding pyrotechnics and giant video screens began to play an increasing role in rock performance. Acts like Kiss ("Detroit Rock City," **Peter Criss**) and Alice Cooper ("I'm Eighteen," **Neal Smith**) painted their faces, dressed in elaborate costumes, and shocked audiences with extreme exploits like spitting blood, breathing fire and self-mutilation. Queen ("Bohemian Rhapsody," **Roger Taylor**) and Electric Light Orchestra ("Evil Woman," **Bev Bevan**) supported majestically produced albums with performances that bordered on Wagnerian spectacles. Pink Floyd, in touring its blockbuster LP *The Wall*, constructed (and subsequently destroyed) an enormous brick wall between band and audience each night.

Despite the new heights achieved by these bands in grand scale entertainment, the seventies saw rock'n'roll start to lose some of the groundbreaking creativity that had characterized it in previous decades. For one thing, it was getting more difficult for musicians to find territory that had not already been explored. Second, rock was now considered a highly profitable commodity, and record companies were becoming less inclined to potentially jeopardize that commodity in the name of artistic freedom.

In general, seventies rock drumming matched the music of the era in both size and scope. Extended drum solos had become a part of most rock concerts, and for the first time in the genre's history, drummers were flaunted from atop their own risers. The explosive popularity of hard rock mandated larger drums, thicker head options and heavier hardware, all designed to withstand the punishment being meted out by a generation trying to imitate John Bonham. By mid-decade, massive drum kits – marked by twin bass drums, multiple tom-toms and endless rows of cymbals - were *de rigueur*. These kits were complimented by new innovations such as concert toms (which featured only a top head), Remo Roto-toms (which could be pitch adjusted by spinning the drum), and Tama Octobans (small tubular tom-toms which came in a set and were melodically tuned). The North drum company shook up the industry briefly with a radical horn-shaped drum set that was designed to project its sound outward. By the late seventies, electric drum pads had also started to feature in many drummers' set ups.

Recording concepts such as close micing and overdubbing, and post-production effects like reverb and delay had given producers and recording engineers inordinate control in the creation of the final product. In exercising that control, they often eliminated the organic sound of drums, preferring to "create" it after the fact. As a result, drums were often heavily taped or otherwise muffled, and often recorded with one head removed. This tended to give the drums on 1970s recordings a very dry, unnatural sound, and had the negative side effect of creating a generation of drummers unable to tune their own instrument.

Still, a great many artists of the seventies (who today make up the bulk of the "classic rock" radio format) managed to successfully define the rock genre in their own image. The sleazy boogie of Aerosmith ("Walk This Way," **Joey Kramer**), the distinctively minimalist grooves of AC/DC ("Highway to Hell," **Phil Rudd**), the eclectic pop of Elton John ("Burn Down the Mission," **Barry Morgan, Roger Pope, Nigel Olsson**), the rough emotion of Supertramp ("Dreamer," **Bob Benberg**), and the straight ahead sound of Bad Company ("Can't Get Enough of Your Love," **Simon Kirke**) all provide solid examples of seventies rock. Other classic seventies rockers include Foghat ("Slow Ride," **Roger Earl**), Blue Öyster Cult ("Don't Fear the Reaper," **Albert Bouchard**), Cheap Trick ("Surrender," **Bun E. Carlos**) and Heart ("Magic Man," **Michael Derosier**).

Later in the decade, a generation of so-called "arena rock" bands stormed the charts with a style that was even more commercially oriented and radio-friendly. Groups like Fleetwood Mac ("Say You Love Me," **Mick Fleetwood**), Foreigner ("Feels Like the First Time," **Dennis Elliot**), Boston ("More Than a Feeling," **John "Sib" Hashian**), Journey ("Wheel in the Sky," **Steve Smith**), Styx ("Come Sail Away," **John Panozzo**), and REO Speedwagon ("Riding the Storm Out," **Alan Gratzer**) all released highly successful albums that boasted slick production featuring anthemic choruses, virtuoso guitar solos and tight vocal harmonies.

Other Major Rock Trends of the Seventies

In the tradition of Bob Dylan, Van Morrison and the Band, the image of the singer-songwriter *cum* rocker also gained popularity in the 1970s. One of the most influential voices of the decade was Bruce Springsteen ("Born to Run"), who was hailed for bringing together all the exuberance of fifties rock with the thoughtfulness of sixties rock, and molding it into a seventies style. In drummer **Max Weinberg**, "the Boss" found a kindred spirit whose roots influences, vintage-style drums and wide-open feel complemented Springsteen's odes to working class America. Over the years, Weinberg would become a strong proponent for educating rock drummers about their roots, releasing a book (*The Big Beat: Conversations With Rock's Great Drummers*), and a series of drum-feature compilations (*Max Weinberg Presents: Let There Be Rock, Vols. 1-3*). Weinberg also styled his house band on *Late Night With Conan O'Brien* in the vein of a classic rhythm and blues combo.

Other "heartland" rockers who drew from the rootsier side of American music include Southside Johnny and the Asbury Jukes ("Hearts of Stone," **Steve Becker**), the J. Geils Band ("Give It To Me," **Stephen Jo Bladd**), Tom Petty ("Don't Do Me Like That," **Stan Lynch**), and John (Cougar) Mellencamp ("Hurt So Good," **Kenny Aronoff**).

Elements of jazz, soul and r&b also found their way into seventies rock, particularly in the horn-inflected sound of Chicago ("Make Me Smile," **Danny Seraphine**) and Blood, Sweat and Tears ("Spinnin' Wheel," **Bobby Colomby**).

"Southern rock," another offshoot that was influential in the early and mid-seventies, drew from the heavy blues-rock of the late sixties as well as honky-tonk and Bakersfield country. Pioneering the genre was the Allman Brothers Band ("One Way Out," **Butch Trucks** and **"Jaimoe" Johnny Johanson**), a double drummer outfit that elaborated on the improvisational tendencies and loudness of Cream and the Grateful Dead while staying closer to rock & roll's blues and country roots. The Allmans were followed shortly by Lynyrd Skynyrd ("Free Bird," **Artemis Pyle**), who played heavier and louder and were notorious for their triple guitar attack. These two bands set the template for all the Southern rock bands that followed, notably Molly Hatchet ("Flirtin' With Disaster," **Bruce Crump**), the Outlaws ("Green Grass and High Tides," **Monte Yoho**), and .38 Special ("Rockin' Into the Night," **Jack Grondin** and **Steve Brookins**). The Dixie Dregs ("Night of the Living Dregs," **Rod Morgenstein**) combined the odd time signatures and complex improvisation of jazz-fusion with the country-fried rock of the South, and landing somewhere between Southern rock and New Orleans funk/r&b was the great Little Feat ("Dixie Chicken"), which featured drummer **Richie Hayward**, a noted session vet who recorded hits with the likes of Steven Stills ("Love the One You're With") and Arlo Guthrie ("City of New Orleans").

In addition to the many solid craftsmen already mentioned, the seventies also had its share of drumming mavericks that advanced rock'n'roll to new technical and artistic heights:

As part of the power trio Rush, **Neil Peart** managed to combine the grand scale of progressive rock with the rooted earnestness of pop to win a cult following that has filled arenas for over three decades. A series of quasi-concept albums like *2112*, *Farewell to Kings* and *Permanent Waves*, gave Peart (who is also Rush's primary lyricist) the forum to develop his extremely precise approach, flawlessly executed via an enormous kit that included glockenspiel, temple blocks, chimes and gongs. In the eighties, this set up would expand to include a full electronic kit, which was often integrated into the drummer's solo feature, "YYZ." With the death of John Bonham in 1980, Peart picked up the torch as perhaps the most influential drummer in rock.

Through his work with artists like Frank Zappa (*Zoot Allures*), U.K. (*Night After Night*), Jeff Beck (*Guitar Shop*), and Missing Persons (a band he co-led, *Spring Session M*), **Terry Bozzio** proved to be one of the more interesting and original rock drummers of the seventies and eighties. He often played untraditional set ups - an all roto-tom kit for example - and his interest in gear led to his patenting several drum-oriented products such as "Spoxe." Stylistically, Bozzio treated his drum set as a tool for orchestration as much as groove playing, and in the 1980s, he developed a "super-independence" which allowed him to freely improvise while simultaneously maintaining complex rhythmic ostinato patterns. Later in his career, Bozzio took this concept further, performing solo drum concerts or duets with other like-minded players such as **Chad Wackerman**.

Finally, it should be noted that after a decade away from the concert stage, Elvis Presley returned to touring in 1969, remaining one of the country's top draws until his death in 1977. This is a remarkable achievement, considering that none of Presley's contemporaries from the early days of rock'n'roll ever came close to reviving their careers to such a degree. Although Elvis' 1970s band was presented more as a Vegas revue than the typical arena rock act, it included many top-notch players, among them the fine drummer **Ron Tutt**. In addition to recording Elvis classics like "Suspicious Minds," Tutt was a major presence in the seventies rock scene, playing on a slew of hit singles - among them Cher's "Gypsies, Tramps and Thieves" and Billy Joel's "Piano Man" - and touring with a variety of rock acts including the Jerry Garcia Band, Delaney and Bonnie, Johnny Rivers and Neil Diamond.

Studio Giants and Journeymen Rockers of the Seventies

One of the biggest musical influences in the 1970s was the so-called "West Coast" sound, a country and folk-tinged form of rock that had initially found favor the previous decade with LA-based groups like the Byrds and the Flying Burrito Brothers. The seventies version of West

Coast rock was epitomized by the Eagles ("Take It Easy," **Don Henley**), America ("A Horse With No Name," **Dave Attwood**), Jackson Brown ("Running on Empty," **Jim Gordon, Russ Kunkel**), Crosby, Stills and Nash ("Suite: Judy Blue Eyes," **Dallas Taylor**), and the double-drummer powered Doobie Brothers ("Taking It To the Streets," **John Hartman** and **Keith Knudsen**).

The popularity of the West Coast sound evidenced a new sophistication in rock music, one that centered around the Los Angeles studio scene, and the highly specialized musicians therein. In the tradition of pioneers like Hal Blaine, a new generation of studio drummer had evolved to help define this sophisticated sound. Having studied the achievements of the Wrecking Crew, these players cut their teeth on the plentiful demo work that was to be had in the pre-sequencing world of the sixties and seventies. Collectively, they would be part of a golden age of record-making.

With a career that has spanned four decades at the time of this writing (and shows no sign of slowing down), **Jim Keltner** stands as the most influential of this new generation. A master at submerging his personality into each track that he records, Keltner has amassed a gold star resume that includes superstars from a variety of genres. He was a personal favorite of three out of four Beatles, touring and recording with John Lennon (*Imagine*, *Mind Games*), George Harrison (*The Concert for Bangladesh*, *All Things Must Pass*), and Ringo Starr (the two double-drummed on hits like "Photograph" and "Oh My My"). Keltner was also featured on hits by Bob Dylan ("Knockin' on Heaven's Door"), Joe Cocker ("Delta Lady"), and Randy Newman ("Short People"). Since the seventies, he has been the drummer of choice for literally hundreds of artists, notably Leon Russell, B.B. King, James Taylor, Elvis Costello, Roy Orbison, Eric Clapton, Brian Wilson, Tom Petty, and Sheryl Crow, as well as numerous all-star projects like the Travelling Wilburys and Little Village.

Cut from the same Palmer/Blaine heritage as Jim Keltner (and actually preceding him by several years) was another West Coast studio legend, **Jim Gordon**. Gordon's drumming was featured on some of the biggest hits of the late sixties (like Mason Williams' "Classical Gas"), and he recorded with many of the decades' most influential artists, among them the Beach Boys (*Pet Sounds*), Derek and the Dominos ("Layla"), Eric Clapton ("After Midnight"), and Joe Cocker ("A Little Help From My Friends"). Gordon also played on many hits of the 1970s, such as John Denver's "Thank God I'm a Country Boy," Johnny Rivers' "Rockin' Pneumonia and the Boogie Woogie Flu," Carly Simon's "You're So Vain" and Gordon Lightfoot's "Sundown."

Russ Kunkel brought his relaxed feel to countless hits as well, personifying in rhythm the laid back feel of West Coast rock. His credits include Joni Mitchell ("Big Yellow Taxi"), James Taylor ("Fire and Rain"), Linda Rondstadt ("You're No Good"), Seals and Crofts ("Summer Breeze"), Carly Simon ("Mockingbird"), Carole King ("I Feel the Earth Move") and CSN ("Dark Star").

Jeff Porcaro's solid, joyful groove was the perfect accompaniment to the slickly produced pop/rock that defined the late seventies and eighties. From his first gig as the 17-year old house drummer on TV's *Sonny & Cher Comedy Hour* until his untimely death in 1992, it is no exaggeration to say that the sound of mainstream pop/rock drumming was, to a large extent, his sound. Porcaro was a hit-maker extraordinaire, and his credits include Seals and Crofts ("Diamond Girl"), John Sebastian ("Welcome Back"), Boz Scaggs ("Lido Shuffle"), and Michael McDonald ("I Keep Forgettin'"). He was also a major fixture on several key Steely Dan records (*Pretzel Logic*, *Katy Lied* and *Gaucho)*, and was co-leader and composer for the Grammy-award winning Toto ("Hold the Line," "Roseanna," "Africa").

Although he was not based on the West Coast, one drummer who left an indelible mark on studio recording in the 1970s is **Steve Gadd**. Best known for the fiery jazz and fusion he played with the likes of Chick Corea (*Friends*, *Three Quartets*) and Al DiMeola (*Elegant Gypsy*), Gadd also made significant contributions in funk, r&b and pop/rock. His subtle but solidly grounded style can be heard on everything from rock oriented hit TV themes (*S.W.A.T.* and *Taxi*), to hits by Kenny Loggins ("I Believe in Love") and Art Garfunkel ("What a Wonderful World"). Definitive Gadd grooves include the funkified march beat of Paul Simon's "50 Ways to Leave Your Lover," the four-stick *Mozambique* of Simon's "Late In the Evening," and the half time funk of Rickie Lee Jones' "Chuck E.'s in Love." Today, Gadd continues to make an impact in the rock world, particularly in the form of large-scale tours with the likes of Simon and Garfunkel, Eric Clapton and James Taylor.

Interestingly, the band that set a high mark for 1970s studio production was not really a band at all. Steely Dan was formed by the eccentric songwriting team of Donald Fagan and Walter Becker, who surrounded themselves with the best studio musicians to create records that were state of the art sonic experiences. Based solely on the quality of these records, Steely Dan was able to secure major airplay and sell millions of units without ever mounting a significant tour (although they did start touring regularly in the early 1990s). Becker and Fagan were notorious for being extremely picky in the studio - they were among of the first to use click tracks extensively - but they also utilized the individual strengths of their players to give each song its own unique character. Memorable Steely Dan drumming moments include **Steve Gadd**'s one-take solo on "Aja", **Bernard "Pretty" Purdie**'s signature half-time funk shuffle on "Babylon Sisters" and "Home At Last," **Rick Marotta**'s "backward" groove on "The Royal Scam," and **Jeff Porcaro**'s jazz waltz on "Gold Teeth II." Two other contributors to Steely Dan's pristine productions were **Jim Hodder** ("Reelin' In the Years") and **Jim Gordon** ("Rikki Don't Lose That Number").

Other drummers who made important contributions to seventies rock, both in the studio and onstage include: **Alan White** (John Lennon, George Harrison, Joe Cocker), **Aynsley Dunbar** (Jeff Beck, Journey, David Bowie, Jefferson Starship), **Kenny Buttrey** (Bob Dylan, Neil Young,

Jimmy Buffet, Gordon Lightfoot), **John Barbata** (the Turtles, CSN, Jefferson Starship), **Tommy Aldridge** (Black Oak Arkansas, Pat Travers, Ozzy Osbourne, Whitesnake), **Rick Marotta** (Al Kooper, Hall and Oates, Jim Croce, Paul Simon, James Taylor), **Simon Phillips** (Jeff Beck, Pete Townsend, Mick Jagger), **Ed Greene** (The Mamas and the Papas, Hall and Oates, Three Dog Night), **Gerry Conway** (Cat Stevens, Fairport Convention, Jethro Tull), **Jamie Oldaker** (Eric Clapton, Peter Frampton, Bob Seger), **Cozy Powell** (Jeff Beck, Rainbow, Michael Schenker Group), **Anton Fig** (Kiss, Bob Dylan, Cyndi Lauper, Mick Jagger, David Letterman House Band), **Andy Newmark** (Carly Simon, Sly and the Family Stone, George Harrison, David Bowie), **Gary Mallabar** (Van Morrison, Steve Miller, Warren Zevon) and **Tris Imboden** (Kenny Loggins, Firefall, Michael McDonald, Chicago).

Punk Rock: Back to the Basics

Although the seventies had been a decade of tremendous growth for rock'n'roll, they were also marked by excess and self-indulgence, both on the part of artists and the labels that promoted them. Bloated production styles, over the top theatrics and gimmicky promotion had come to dominate the genre, the end product of an increasingly commercialized marketplace. There was a growing perception - especially among the younger generation - that rock'n'roll and other heavily saturated styles like disco were less about music than the almighty dollar.

Disaffection with what was labeled "corporate rock" boiled over in a backlash that became known as punk. Although punk rock remained an underground phenomenon until the 1990s, it completely changed the face of the music industry, and its offspring (post-punk and new wave) were the first to take full advantage of the MTV phenomenon.

On a musical level, punk returned rock & roll to the basics - three chords and a simple melody – and it did it louder, faster and more abrasively than any other rock & roll in the past. But punk also twisted and distorted the traditional pop format. Many punk songs ran less than two minutes, and were often accompanied by radical transitions and abrupt endings. Punk was also marked by a strong political component, characterized by calls for anarchy and by a distinctively "anti-fashion" statement comprised of ripped t-shirts, combat boots, Mohawk haircuts and facial piercings. Contrary to the grandiose aspirations of seventies rock, punk bands focused on a lo-fi, homemade approach to recording, and many still manufacture their music on vinyl to this day.

Punk developed in the mid-seventies, with separate scenes developing simultaneously on both sides of the Atlantic. In New York, the first punk band was the Ramones, whose bubble gum garage-inspired anthems like "Blitzkrieg Bop" and "I Wanna Be Sedated" referenced sixties girl groups and the New York Dolls. The band's drummers - **Tommy Ramone**, followed by **Marky Ramone** – both laid down a solid, straightforward approach that set the tone for the entire punk drumming tradition. Other important bands that defined the New York punk scene - via

41

appearances at low brow clubs like CBGB's - include the Velvet Underground-inspired Television ("Marquee Moon," **Billy Ficca**), the goulish Misfits ("I Stand Alone," **Joey Damage**) and the arty Talking Heads ("Psycho Killer," **Chris Frantz**).

Across the Atlantic, the Sex Pistols (**Paul Cook**) emerged out of working class London, where punk would become a full-scale social movement. When they appeared in 1976, the Pistols gave voice to the rage of the lower class and the dissatisfaction of the nation's youth. Through raw, nihilistic singles ("God Save the Queen," "Holiday in the Sun," "Bodies") and often violent performances, the band revolutionized the idea of what rock & roll could be. In England, the group was considered dangerous to the very fabric of society and was banned across the country. However, the sheer sonic force of their music inspired the formation of other British punk bands like the Clash ("London Calling," **Topper Headon**), the Buzzcocks ("What Do I Get," **John Maher**), the Jam ("The Modern World," **Rick Buckler**), the Damned ("New Rose," **Rat Scabies**), and Joy Division ("Love Will Tear Us Apart," **Stephen Morris**). Countless other groups in both the U.S. and the U.K. were inspired by the Pistol's independent, do-it-yourself ethics, giving rise to the massive independent music underground in both countries.

In the early eighties, Los Angeles established itself as the center for the next phase of punk, a faster, more aggressive version known as hardcore. West coast bands that pioneered the hardcore style include Black Flag ("Rise Above," **Robo**), the Circle Jerks ("Wild In the Streets," **Lucky Lehrer**), the Germs ("Forming," **Don Bolles**), the Dead Kennedys ("Holiday in Cambodia," **Ted**, later **D.H. Peligro**), and Fear ("Let's Have a War," **Spit Stix**). The West coast also fostered the birth of pioneering indie punk labels like SST, Epitaph and Alternative Tentacles. In successfully signing some of the most important punk and alternative bands of the eighties and nineties, these labels demonstrated that an independent underground subculture could succeed financially outside the corporate environment of the music industry.

Another initial form of punk was straight-edge, a highly political style based upon a rigorous drug free, vegetarian lifestyle, and espoused by groups like Minor Threat ("Out of Step," **Jeff Nelson**) and Fugazi ("Suggestion," **Brendan Canty**). Bad Brains ("I Against I," **Earl Hudson**) – one of the few African-American punk groups - combined punk with reggae, while various "skinhead" punk bands brought extreme elements like Nazism into their music. As opposed to other styles of rock, punk boasted a large number of bands fronted by women, among them Patti Smith, X, and Blondie. And starting with **Sandy West** of the all-female unit the Runaways, punk laid claim to its own cadre of talented female drummers, notably the Go-Go's **Elissa Bello** (later **Gina Shock**), and the Bangles' **Vicki Peterson**.

Stylistic differences aside, punk drumming on the whole represented a return to rock's most basic objective, where raw emotion was the driving force as opposed to polished technique and perfect time. In keeping with this philosophy, early punk recordings feature a no-frills drum sound: extremely dry, with thin, papery crashes. Since one of punk's goals was to express chaos and discord, drum grooves were often played so fast that the time signature was either lost or completely indistinguishable. And as most punk drummers had little technique or professional experience, few became stars among the community at large. Punk did, however, have its share of stylists, among them **Bill Stevenson** (Black Flag, Descendents, All), **D.J. Bonebrake** (X), **Chuck Biscuits** (D.O.A., Danzig, Social Distortion), **Sim Cain** (Gone, Rollins Band), and **Bobby Schayer** (Bad Religion).

New Wave: Punk Goes Pop

New Wave was a catch-all term for the more commercial music that directly followed punk in the late seventies and eighties. While post-punk styles like hardcore retained the music's more radical elements (political lyrics, mosh pits), new wave was pop music, pure and simple. It retained the vigor and irreverence of punk music, but also indulged in a fascination with electronics, style, and art.

New wave incorporated a wide variety of acts, from edgy songwriters like Elvis Costello ("Pump It Up," **Pete Thomas**) and Joe Jackson ("Is She Really Going Out With Him," **Gary Burke**), to rock revivalists like Graham Parker ("White Honey," **Steve Goulding**), and mainstream rockers like Blondie ("Heart of Glass," **Clem Burke**), the Pretenders ("Tattooed Love Boys," **Martin Chambers**), Squeeze ("Pulling Muscles From a Shell," **Gilson Lavis**), Nick Lowe ("Cruel To Be Kind, **Terry Williams**), the Cars ("Just What I Needed," **David Robinson**) and U2 ("I Will Follow," **Larry Mullen Jr.**). Despite the stylistic diversity among these acts, they all shared a love of pop hooks, modernist style and a fascination for being slightly left of center.

Ska, roots reggae and the emerging sound of dub also played a large role in the sound of punk and new wave, particularly in England, which was home to a large Jamaican immigrant community. Bands like the Clash ("Bank Robber"), XTC ("Making Plans for Nigel") and Joe Jackson ("Sunday Papers") made great use of the cross-stick backbeats, timbale-esque fills, and tight offbeat hi hat patterns first popularized in the 1960s by Jamaican groups like the Skatalites (**Lloyd Nibbs**). By the early eighties, ska-inflected punk had grown into a full fledged genre of its own, with multi-racial groups like the Specials ("A Message to You Rudy," **John Bradbury**), the English Beat ("Mirror In the Bathroom," **Everett Moreton**), Madness ("One Step Beyond," **Dan Woodgate**), and the Selecter ("On My Radio," **Compton Amanor**) having mainstream success in both England and America. A variation of the juba rhythm known as the "Burundi Beat" colored the hits of several English new wave groups, particularly Adam and the Ants ("Dog Eat Dog," **Merrick**) and Bow Wow Wow ("I Want Candy," **David Barbarossa**).

In 1978, the Police exploded on the scene to become one of the most popular bands of the post-punk era. Their earliest successes - "I Can't Stand Losing You," "Message In A Bottle," and "Walking on the Moon" – were all based in the ska/reggae influence of the period, and featured the incredibly inventive drumming of **Stewart Copeland**. Copeland combined a clean, hard-hitting style with a distinctive set up that featured a cranked snare, pitched Octoban tom-toms and an assortment of splash cymbals. He continued to refine that style on later tracks like "Spirits In the Material World," "Every Little Thing She Does Is Magic" and "Murder By Numbers," and by the mid-eighties was considered one of the most influential drummers in all of rock. With the breakup of the Police in 1983, Copeland (who is related to American classical composer Aaron Copeland) became an established composer in his own right, writing soundtracks (*Rumble Fish*), recording imaginative solo albums (*The Rhythmatist*), and co-leading adventurous groups (Animal Logic).

The rise of new wave also firmly established the synthesizer as a mainstream element in rock'n'roll. As the main component of mechanized "synth-pop" groups like Gary Numan ("Cars," **Jess Lidyard**) and "new romantics" like Duran Duran ("Hungry Like the Wolf," **Roger Taylor**), the synthesizer would be heavily featured in MTV's first generation of videos. Goth rock, a new wave offshoot that relied heavily on synthesized production, was typified by Bauhaus ("Bela Lugosi is Dead," **Kevin Haskins**), the Cure ("Boys Don't Cry," **Laurence Tolhurst**) and Siouxsie and the Banshees ("Christine," **Budgie**). Industrial rock, yet another technology-driven style to emerge around the time of punk, endeavored to express rock as a reflection of the mechanized world of the late 20th century. Early industrial bands like Throbbing Gristle adopted a performance art approach, while eighties pioneers like Skinny Puppy (**cEVIN Key**) and Ministry (**William Rieflin**) combined sequenced drum beats with heavy metal power chords to create a bleak, punishing sonic landscape.

As the eighties unfolded, drum machines, electronic pads, samples and triggering would play an increasingly dominant role in rock music production, putting new demands on drummers to integrate electronic technology into what had always been an acoustic artform. The decade also saw an increased popularity of foreign drum makers like Pearl, Yamaha, Tama, and Sonor, whose ultra modern image blended perfectly with the technology-obsessed eighties.

Chapter Four: The Eighties

On the whole, eighties rock'n'roll veered away significantly from the wide-open state of affairs that had characterized the sixties and seventies. Rock was no longer distinguished by the influence of the blues, and gone were the free form improvisations that had once been so prevalent. The immediacy of punk and new wave had made jam-heavy styles like progressive rock and fusion seem like overblown dinosaurs, and even the world's biggest hard rock acts had to rethink their approach. CDs replaced LPs and cassettes, drastically altering the nature in which music was presented. The eighties also saw a period of consolidation within the music industry, one in which many record companies were bought out by large conglomerates whose financial bottom line far outweighed artistic considerations. This meant that labels were less likely to sign artists that did not fit into already commercially proven categories.

The Evolution of Metal

Nowhere were these changes more evident than in the world of heavy metal, which had been becoming progressively formulaic since the late seventies. A cache of European bands including UFO, ("Lights Out," **Andy Parker**), the Scorpians ("Lovedrive," **Herman Rareball**), Judas Priest ("Hell Bent For Leather," **Les Binks**), Iron Maiden ("Wrathchild," **Clive Burr**, later **Nico McBrain**), and Motorhead ("Ace of Spades," **"Philthy Animal" Taylor**) emerged during this period with a faster, leaner, and more menacing version of the music originated by Led Zeppelin and Black Sabbath. Although the music was credible and interesting, it was more stereotyped and predictable than its predecessors, and was marked by much more precise, consistent parts.

The flashy guitar leads and wild party rock of Van Halen ("You Really Got Me," **Alex Van Halen)** and Ozzy Osbourne ("Crazy Train," **Tommy Aldridge**, later **Randy Castillo**) gave metal an even more polished look, kicking off an era where it would enjoy its greatest presence on the charts. A group of glammed-up "hair-metal" bands led by Mötley Crüe ("Shout at the Devil," **Tommy Lee**), Def Leppard ("Pyromania," **Rick Allen**), Poison ("Same Old Situation," **Rikki Rocket**) and Guns'n'Roses ("Welcome to the Jungle," **Steven Adler**, later **Matt Sorum**) were the primary beneficiaries of this success. Relying on the seventies glam image and a sound based in Led Zeppelin, Aerosmith and the Rolling Stones, these bands sold millions of records and took arena rock production to new levels, but generated relatively little in the way of cutting edge rock'n'roll.

As a reaction to metal's mainstream pop breakthrough, an American metal scene known as thrash also took shape in the eighties. Thrash bands played complex riffs at breakneck speed, sometimes dispensing with vocal melody altogether. Thrash was the domain of Metallica (*Kill 'Em All*, *Ride the Lightening*), easily the best and most influential heavy metal band of the entire decade. With dense layers of production, myriad odd time signatures, and gruff, monotone vocals Metallica used speed and volume not for their own sake, but to enhance their intricately structured compositions. Drummer **Lars Ulrich** took metal drumming to new levels of sophistication, particularly in his contributions to the bass drum. By using wood as opposed to felt bass drum beaters, Ulrich was able to create a compressed, attack-heavy sound that managed to retain the depth of the drum. And rather than follow in the metal tradition of using two bass drums to create a steady stream of eighth notes, Ulrich ingeniously expressed his double bass patterns as tightly wound bursts that were intricately woven into each song's overall character. On the band's early recordings, he rarely if ever used a ride cymbal.

Throughout the eighties, Metallica built a rabid cult following, inspiring the even harder variations of speed and death metal. Megadeath ("Wake Up Dead," **Gar Samuelson**, later **Chuck Behler**, then **Nick Menza**) combined extremely fast, clean grooves with elements of fusion, while Slayer ("Seasons in the Abyss," **Dave Lombardo**) intoned grim, brutal odes to death, serial killers, and Satanism. Pantera ("Walk," **Vinnie Paul**) featured a melodic aural assault of power chords and growling "Cookie Monster" vocals, while Brazil's Sepultura ("Ratamahatta," **Igor Cavalera**) was one of the first metal bands to attract a punk rock audience.

Alternative Rock

By the mid-eighties, post-punk had morphed into alternative rock, which ended the dominance of synth-driven new wave and fueled a back-to-the-garage movement in the American underground. Supported by the rapidly growing college radio format, groups like R.E.M. ("Radio Free Europe," "Catapult") combined ringing hooks with cryptic lyrics to bring stripped down guitar-pop back into the underground lexicon. Though there were no overt innovations to his drumming, **Bill Berry**'s unadorned and straightforward style gave R.E.M. a candor that simultaneously sounded traditional and modern.

Other guitar-driven alternative bands like Hüsker Dü ("Turn On the News," **Grant Hart**), the Minutemen ("It's Expected I'm Gone," **George Hurley**), Sonic Youth ("Expressway to Yr. Skull," **Steve Shelley**) the Meat Puppets ("Up on the Sun," **Derrick Bostrom**), the Pixies ("Bone Machine," **David Lovering**), the Replacements ("I Will Dare," **Chris Mars**), and Dinosaur Jr. ("Sludgefest," **Murph**) combined R.E.M's spartan edge with elements of hardcore punk and experimental noise. English rock also re-embraced the guitar with a group of hit makers led by the Smiths ("How Soon Is It Now," **Mike Joyce**), and the Stone Roses ("I Wanna Be Adored," **Reni**).

After spending decades as the domain of mostly white artists and audiences, the eighties saw a number of highly successful African-American rock groups cross the color line. Prince, who based his image on classic rockers like Little Richard, James Brown and Jimi Hendrix, fused rock with soul, funk and r&b on hit albums like *Purple Rain* ("Let's Go Crazy," **Bobby Z.**). He also consistently featured talented female musicians, notably drummer **Sheila E.** (*Sign of the Times*). The eighties also saw the successful debut of African-American funk-rocker Lenny Kravitz, who played the drums on all his recordings ("Let Love Rule," toured with **Zoro**, later **Cindy Blackman**), and the eclectic band Living Color ("Cult of Personality," **Will Calhoun**). Both of these acts attracted a primarily white audience from the start. Finally, the British ska revival influenced the rise of similarly inclined multi-racial bands stateside, the most important being the Untouchables ("Agent Double O Soul," **Willie McNeil**) and Fishbone ("Fight the Youth," **Phil Fisher**).

A Revival of Rock's Roots

Although the rock music of the seventies and eighties appeared to have left behind the majority of its musical connection to the 1950s, the "roots" elements of blues, r&b and rockabilly that once defined the genre never disappeared completely from the radar screen. Many of rock's originators, particularly Chuck Berry, Little Richard, Bo Diddley, Bill Haley, and Jerry Lee Lewis, had continued performing, despite being considered out of fashion. Aided by some long overdue recognition from the British Invaders and others, these artists were all in the process of making a comeback of one sort or another by the early seventies.

At the same time, a new generation of rockers dedicated to the traditional American roots styles were also gaining popularity. Sha Na Na ("Rock'n'Roll Is Here to Stay"), had made a splash at the 1969 Woodstock festival with their tribute to fifties rock'n'roll, and they parlayed that success into a very popular TV variety show in the seventies. Other bands like Commander Cody ("Hot Rod Lincoln," **Lance Dickerson)**, NRBQ ("Howard Johnson's Got His Ho Jo Working," **Tom Staley**, later **Tommy Ardolino**), Roomful of Blues ("Okie Dokie Stomp," **John Rossi**) and Asleep at the Wheel ("Take Me Back to Tulsa," **Lucky Oceans**, later **David Sanger**) enjoyed significant cult success with their celebration of traditional styles like jump blues, rockabilly and Western swing. The 1974 release of *American Graffiti*, followed by the phenomenally successful TV show *Happy Days*, instigated a full-blown fifties revival (albeit one that was somewhat sugar coated in nostalgia).

That roots revival reached a peak of sorts in the 1980s, when a variety of younger bands earned mainstream success playing older styles of rock. George Thorogood ("Bad To The Bone," **Jeff Simon**) became a mainstay on MTV with his accessible output of Chuck Berry-style blues. And the Stray Cats wedded the ethos of punk and new wave to the rockabilly swagger of Eddie Cochran and Gene Vincent to score big with hits like "Stray Cat Strut" and "Rock This Town." Standing up behind a two-piece cocktail-style kit, Cats drummer **Slim Jim Phantom** gave the classic shuffles of rockabilly and early rock a high-octane transfusion that allowed the Stray Cats' music to fit right in with other hits of the day. British pub-rock acts like Rockpile (**Terry Williams**) also integrated the rockabilly sound and style, and hard rock vets like Queen ("Crazy Little Thing Called Love") and Led Zeppelin frontman Robert Plant – with his side project The Honeydrippers ("Rockin' at Midnight") - enjoyed roots-inspired hits in the eighties as well. Along with other revival trends like Ska, rockabilly would become a permanent fixture on the underground music scene, attracting new devotees with every successive generation.

Stevie Ray Vaughn - building on the attention he received as David Bowie's guitarist on 1982 smash *Let's Dance* (which featured the superb drumming of **Omar Hakim** and **Tony Thompson**) - was responsible for a renewed interest in the blues. A reincarnation of the classic

Texas troubadour, Vaughn employed an incendiary style that was reminiscent of a number of legendary guitarists, from Albert King to Jimi Hendrix. Vaughn's drummer, **Chris Layton**, revealed a similar mastery, and the resonant double shuffles and laid-back funk work he employed on recordings like "Texas Flood" and "Couldn't Stand the Weather" reintroduced a traditional blues feel that had been absent from the mainstream for decades. Steve Ray Vaughn was the biggest name in a strong Austin, TX based music scene that saw a variety of roots artists cross over into the mainstream, notably Jerry Jeff Walker ("Mr. Bojangles") and the Fabulous Thunderbirds ("Tuff Enuff," **Fran Christina**).

A New Generation of Drumming Supermen

As with each successive decade before it, the 1980s produced a generation of studio drummers that rewrote the book on what was possible for a human being to accomplish behind a drum kit. Forged in the mold created by Billy Cobham, Steve Gadd and Jim Keltner, the drummers of this generation functioned with ease in every musical setting, playing with such precision and advanced technique that their performances seemed almost superhuman. Although their credits tended more toward jazz, fusion, funk, and pop, the following players also had a heavy influence in the rock world:

Vinnie Colaiuta's riotous approach and ferocious technique with Frank Zappa (*Joe's Garage, Shut Up and Play Your Guitar*) quickly established him as a major force in the world of drumming, and led to major session work with the likes of Joni Mitchell (*Wild Things Run Free*), Gino Vanelli (*Nightwalker*) and Billy Joel (*The Bridge*). After a decade of dominating the studio scene, Colaiuta joined Sting in 1990 (*Ten Summoners Tales*) for a six-year stint. Today, he continues to record with all manner of rock artists from Stevie Nicks to Megadeath.

Although he first came to prominence with the arena rock supergroup Journey, **Steve Smith** established himself in the 1980s as one of the foremost exponents of contemporary rock-fusion drumming in the vein of Tony Williams. He was a key factor in reinvigorating the genre at a time when its popularity was at low ebb. Smith's incredible power and ample chops are featured on projects with Jan Hammer, Jeff Berlin, Tony MacAlpine, Steps Ahead, Neal Schon, Frank Gambale and Scott Henderson, as well as with his own group Vital Information (*Vital Information, Global Beat*).

After getting his start in 1979 with George Clinton's P-Funk All-Stars (*Live at the Beverly Theatre in Hollywood*), Cobham-heir apparent **Dennis Chambers** established the credentials to score plum fusion gigs with the likes of John Scofield (*Blue Matter*), Mike Stern (*Jigsaw*), and John McLaughlin (*Tokyo Live*). In the 1990s, Chambers took on a more rock-oriented workload, recording with Steely Dan (*Alive in America*) and Santana (*Shaman*), in addition to working with his own power trio Niacin (*Niacin*).

Kenny Aronoff's clean style of power rock drumming first turned heads when he joined John (Cougar) Mellencamp's band in 1980 ("Jack and Diane," "R.O.C.K. in the USA") for a stint that would last 15 years. During that time, Aronoff's playing also graced hits by Jon Bon Jovi ("Blaze of Glory") and Belinda Carlisle ("Heaven Is a Place On Earth"), and garnered him "first call" status with the likes of Bob Dylan, Bob Seger, Indigo Girls, Meat Loaf, Melissa Etheridge, the Rolling Stones, Joe Cocker, Lynyrd Skynyrd, and John Fogerty.

Dave Weckl exploded on the scene in 1986 with Chick Corea's very popular Elektric Band (*Elektric Band, Eye of the Beholder*), balancing a career as a top sideman with work as a leader, clinician and educator. Since the early nineties, Weckl has released several albums of top jazz-fusion under his own name (*Master Plan, Rhythm of the Soul*), and has been prolific in publishing instructional books and DVDs intended to help decipher the phenomenal technique that has distinguished him as one of drumming's all time greats.

Others who made prominent contributions to rock drumming in the eighties: **Manu Katche** (Peter Gabriel, Sting, Robbie Robertson), **Chad Wackerman** (Frank Zappa, Steve Vai, Albert Lee), **Denny Fongheiser** (Tracy Chapman, Counting Crows, Heart), **Mel Gaynor** (Simple Minds, Joan Armatrading, Elton John), **Carlos Vega** (James Taylor, David Foster, Bonnie Raitt), **John "J.R." Robinson** (Kenny Loggins, Glen Frey, David Lee Roth), **Steve Ferrone** (Average White Band, Eric Clapton, Tom Petty), **Mark Craney** (Jean-Luc Ponty, Gino Vanelli, Jethro Tull), **Johnny "Vatos" Hernandez** (Oingo Boingo), **Charlie Drayton** (Divinyls, Keith Richards, B-52's) **Tom Brechtlein** (Chick Corea, Robben Ford, Al DiMeola) and **Gregg Bissonette** (David Lee Roth, Steve Vai, Gary Hoey).

Chapter Five: The Nineties

A Decade of Hybrids and Revivals

The nineties saw an acceleration of the music business consolidation begun a decade earlier. By the middle of the nineties, a few large conglomerates held a virtual monopoly at nearly every level of the industry, controlling record labels, radio stations, retail outlets and performance venues. Disc jockeys in commercial radio formats, no longer allowed to program their own music, field requests or introduce new bands, were reduced to the status of "on-air personalities." With multi-platinum mega-hits needed to fuel this enormous system, the corporate climate depended more than ever on "one hit wonders" to drive sales. As a result, radio formats narrowed increasingly, their playlists loaded with middle-of-the-road acts calculated to appeal to the most general of tastes. Not surprisingly, these practices were detrimental to rock music as a whole, not only because they stifled innovation, but also because they prevented artists from building meaningful, long-term careers.

Still, the nineties did see some interesting trends in rock develop, mostly in the form of hybrids which brought rock together with a variety of other musical staples. And perhaps because the end of a century is often marked by a review of the past, the nineties also saw a revisiting of many styles that had been popular throughout the 20th century.

In the case of the former, many nineties rockers began to integrate rap and hip-hop into their music, a practice that dated to 1986 when Run-DMC teamed up with Aerosmith for their cover of the classic "Walk This Way." In the late eighties, bands like the Beastie Boys ("So Watcha Want," **Mike D**), the Red Hot Chili Peppers ("Subway to Venus," **Jack Irons**, later **Chad Smith**), and Faith No More ("We Care a Lot," **Mike Bordin**) began rapping over rock and funk grooves and blending elements as diverse as sampled beats and slap bass with the speed and irreverent attitude of punk and metal. By the early nineties, rap and funk elements were appearing regularly on "modern rock" playlists, employed by bands like Rage Against the Machine ("Killing in the Name," **Brad Wilk**), 311 ("Down," **Chad Sexton**), Korn ("Good God," **David Silveria**), and Kid Rock ("Cowboy," **Stefanie Eulinberg**). In a further nod to the influence of hip-hop, rock bands across the spectrum - from the pop-oriented Sugar Ray ("Fly," **Stan Frazier**) to "rap-core" monsters Limp Bizkit ("Nookie," **John Otto**) - added DJ's to their lineup.

Driven by the success of late eighties bands like Jane's Addiction ("Mountain Song," **Stephen Perkins**) nineties mainstream metal branched out considerably to embrace a wide variety of genre bending acts. Nine Inch Nails ("Closer," **Chris Vrenna**), Marilyn Manson ("The Beautiful People," **Ginger Fish**) and White Zombie ("More Human Than Human," **Ivan de Prume, John Tempesta**) combined grinding thrash with flourishes of industrial, while Primus ("My Name is Mud," **Tim "Herb" Alexander**, later **Brian "Brain" Mantia**) and Tool ("Stinkfist," **Danny Carry**) incorporated elements of experimental and progressive rock to great result. One of the top hard rock acts of the decade was Smashing Pumpkins ("Cherub Rock," **Jimmy Chamberlain**), who helped bring the sound of alternative rock to new mainstream heights, while the Black Crowes ("Hard to Handle," **Steve Gorman**) emanated a seventies-style raunch that was highly reminiscent of the Stones and the Faces.

The Seattle-born "grunge" phenomenon of the early nineties was a back-to-the-garage movement that arose in response to the self-indulgence and pretentiousness of eighties pop metal bands like Gun'n'Roses and Mötley Crüe. In general, grunge bands wrote songs that dealt with social issues as opposed to mindless partying, and modeled a down-to-earth, anti-corporate image that resonated strongly with disenfranchised teens. The Seattle scene yielded some of the decade's most influential drummers, particularly Nirvana's **Dave Grohl** ("Smells Like Teen Spirit,"), who along with other Northwest vets like the Melvins' **Dale Crover** ("Honey Bucket") and

Mudhoney's **Dan Peters** ("Touch Me I'm Sick") reflected deep punk influences. With the suicide of Nirvana guitarist Kurt Cobain, Grohl would go on to lead his own highly successful group, Foo Fighters ("I'll Stick Around," "Everlong"), for which he wrote all the material, played guitar and sang in addition to covering the drum duties.

Other Seattle drummers like Soundgarden's **Matt Cameron** ("Black Hole Sun"), Pearl Jam's **Dave Krusen** ("Alive," later **Dave Abbrusseze, Jack Irons** and **Matt Cameron**), and Alice In Chains' **Sean Kinney** ("Would?") played in a style reminiscent of seventies hard rock. As the decade wore on, grunge as a whole evolved into a more formulaic and radio friendly entity via bands like Hootie and the Blowfish ("Let Her Cry," **Jim "Soni" Sonefeld**), Third Eye Blind ("Semi-Charmed Life," **Brad Hargraves**) and Live ("I Alone," **Chad Gracey**).

In general, grunge had the overall effect of balancing the processed, effect-driven rock production of the eighties by promoting the natural sound of the instruments, particularly the drums. This return to a more organic drum sound also coincided with a newfound appreciation for vintage drums among both players and producers, as well as the rise of American drum companies like Drum Workshop and Gretsch, which endeavored to emphasize the nation's heritage as the birthplace of the drumset.

In addition to grunge, the nineties saw the rise of other rock styles that looked to the past for inspiration. In the tradition of the Grateful Dead, "jam" bands like Phish (*A Picture of Nectar*, **John Fishman**), and Widespread Panic ("Airplane," **Todd Nance**) were able to attract huge cult followings and sell large numbers of records without the benefit of radio airplay. Other jam-oriented bands like Medeski, Martin and Wood ("Lively Up Yourself," **Billy Martin**) came from a jazz perspective, while Galactic ("Go Go," **Stanton Moore**), G. Love and Special Sauce ("Cold Beverage," **Jeff "Houseman" Clemens**) and the Grey Boy All-Stars ("A Town Called Earth," **Zak Najor**) added elements of New Orleans funk and James Brown style syncopation. Acid jazz, an early nineties phenomenon spearheaded by Jamiroquai ("Virtual Insanity," **Derrick McKenzie**) and the Brand New Heavies ("Never Stop," **Jan Kincaid**) also succeeded in blending jazz harmonies and funky grooves into the rock milieu. The Dave Matthews Band, which featured the standout funk/r&b drumming of **Carter Beauford** ("What Would You Say"), garnered significant radio play to emerge as the most commercially successful of these types of bands.

After nearly two decades as an underground movement, punk rock (along with its accompanying image and lifestyle) burst into the mainstream in the mid-nineties, led by a wave of revivalists including Green Day ("Nimrod," **Tré Cool**), Rancid ("Ruby Soho," **Brett Reed**), and the Offspring ("Come Out and Play," **Ron Welty**). Although these bands drew their inspiration from edgy punk pioneers like the Buzzcocks and the Clash, they were soon overtaken by the more commercial sound of "pop punk," which featured made-for-radio teen-oriented groups like Blink-182 ("Dammit," **Scott Raynor**, later **Travis Barker**) and Unwritten Law ("Seein' Red,"

Wade Youman).

The punk revival had its roots primarily in Orange County, California, a region that also inspired other punk hybrid movements, including the so-called "third wave" ska-punk movement. Ska-punk blended the fast tempos of punk with the offbeat "skank" and horn influences common in sixties ska and rocksteady. Spearheaded by a group of SoCal bands including No Doubt ("I'm Just a Girl," **Adrian Young**) and Sublime ("Date Rape," **Bud Gaugh**), the third wave also had million sellers in the Mighty Mighty Bosstones ("The Impression That I Get," **Joe Cirois**) and Reel Big Fish ("Sell Out," **Andrew Gonzales**).

While leading punk's transition to the mainstream, the West Coast managed to simultaneously maintain its tradition of uncompromising hardcore with veteran acts like Bad Religion ("21st Century (Digital Boy)," **Bobby Schayer**) and Social Distortion ("Mommy's Little Monster," **Derek O'Brien**), and newer devotees like Pennywise ("Bro Hymn," **Byron McMackin**) and NOFX ("Bob," **Erik Ghint**). Several female led alternative/punk bands also emerged, notably the Breeders ("Cannonball," **Jim MacPherson**), L7 ("Pretend We're Dead," **Dee Plakas**), Hole ("Doll Parts," **Patty Schemel**), and P.J. Harvey ("Rid of Me," **Robert Ellis**).

In the second half of the nineties, a swing and rhythm and blues revival came out of left field to find huge success among mainstream rock audiences. With roots in the eighties rockabilly and punk scenes, the so-called "retro-swing" phenomenon was kicked off in 1989 by the influential Royal Crown Revue ("Hey Pachuco," **Mark Stern**, later **Daniel Glass**), who sported a classic gangster image, and utilized an old-school instrumentation that included a horn section, hollow body guitar, vintage drums and upright bass. RCR drew its inspiration from the past, but created a "hard-boiled" musical hybrid that resonated with twenty-something audiences. Their success inspired mid-nineties acts like the Squirrel Nut Zippers ("Hell," **Chris Phillips**), the Cherry Poppin' Daddies ("Zoot Suit Riot," **Tim Donahue**) and Big Bad Voodoo Daddy ("You and Me and the Bottle Makes Three," **Kurt Sodergren**) who enjoyed platinum sales as well as airplay on MTV and mainstream rock radio. Former Stray Cat guitarist Brian Setzer fronted a full big band ("Jump, Jive and Wail," **Bernie Dresel**), which peaked the retro-swing movement by winning several Grammy awards. Despite the swing moniker, the drumming employed by all these groups resembled the backbeat shuffles of fifties r&b much more than it did the big band style of the thirties and forties.

Inspired by seventies roots veterans like the Cramps ("Rock on the Moon," **Nick Knox**), several nineties acts like the Reverend Horton Heat ("Wiggle Stick," **Patrick "Taz" Bentley**, later **Scott Churilla**) and Southern Culture on the Skids ("Camel Walk," **Dave Hartman**) also had success updating classic American roots styles, particularly with a punk-tinged brand of rockabilly known as "psychobilly."

Another style that enjoyed a mid-nineties revival was progressive rock, sparked by groups like

Dream Theater (*Images and Words*, **Mike Portnoy**) and Spock's Beard (*The Light*, **Nick D'Virgilio**), whose sound was inspired by Rush and Genesis. The "Brit-pop" tradition lived on as well in a new generation of English guitar-driven bands like Blur ("Girls and Boys," **Dave Rowntree**), Oasis ("Wonderwall," **Alan White**) and the Verve ("Bittersweet Symphony," **Peter Salisbury**). Christian rock - which had periodically broken into the mainstream since the early eighties with bands like Petra (**Louie Weaver**), Stryper (**Robert Sweet**) and King's X (**Jerry Gaskill**) – now boasted its own hard rock, grunge and metal bands capable of filling sizeable venues. And the Latin-American "Rock en Español" movement also became big business in the U.S. via groups like Mexico's Maná (**Alex Gonzáles**), which proved very popular among non-Latino listeners.

Drummers of the nineties who made important contributions to rock include **Mark Schulman** (Simple Minds, Foreiger, Cher), **Curt Bisquera** (Bonnie Raitt, Seal, Whiskey Town), **Matt Chamberlain** (Edie Brickell, Fiona Apple, Tori Amos), **Sterling Campbell** (B-52s, David Bowie, Soul Asylum), **Joey Waronker** (Beck, R.E.M., Tonic, Elliott Smith), **Taylor Hawkins** (Alanis Morisette, Foo Fighters, Brian May), **Josh Freese** (the Vandals, Paul Westerberg, A Perfect Circle), **Brooks Wackerman** (Infectious Grooves, Bad Religion), **Gary Novak** (Alanis Morisette, Alan Holdsworth, Rob Zombie) and **Abe Laboriel Jr.** (Duran Duran, k.d. Lang, Paul McCartney).

Technology Rising

By the mid-nineties, the growing influence of house, techno, and electronica began to have an impact on the world of rock, as artists like Bjork, Moby and Prodigy - using primarily sequenced drums on their recordings – enjoyed mainstream hits. Beck ("Where It's At," **Joey Waronker**), Radiohead ("Creep," **Phil Selway**) and Garbage ("Stupid Girl," **Butch Vig**) all integrated samples, loops and other technology into their music, drawing the sound of rock in a distinctly electronic direction.

Overall, the nineties witnessed a technological revolution that had tremendous consequences for music worldwide. Pro-tools and other digital music editing software, which had become affordable and easy to use, made it possible to create music directly from samples and loops, eliminating the need for a studio or musicians. Many artists saw the concept of electronically based music as a new frontier, and a welcome alternative to an industry that had recycled the same ideas for so many years. As a result, programmed tracks quickly became the production standard in a variety of styles, notably dance music, contemporary r&b/hip-hop and a great deal of pop.

Whether it eliminated musicians or not, programming software's influence extended into every musical genre, primarily because it offered artists and producers a broad range of editing tools and effects, and simultaneously gave them the ability to "clean up" inconsistencies in time-feel and pitch, resulting in "perfect" tracks. As a result of this new emphasis on technology, much of the commercial rock music released in the late nineties was marked by a new kind of hyper-tightness, stripped of the rough "human feel" that had defined it for so long.

As was the case in the technology boom of the early 1980s, drummers became the first casualties of this new transition, suddenly rendered obsolete in a variety of genres. The increased use of editing software also led to significant declines in demo and recording work for drummers in the nineties, and many live music venues disappeared in favor of dance clubs that featured programmed beats. Drummers responded to a degree, learning from and working with the technology to push the envelope as players and craftsmen. **Tony Verderosa**, **Zach Danziger**, and **Johnny Rabb** all published instructional materials showing drummers how to use loops and samples within their own milieu, and demonstrating ways to imitate the sped up syncopated grooves and mechanical sounds of styles like techno and drum'n'bass. The late nineties also saw the emergence of a new generation of virtuosos like **Virgil Donati, Marco Minnemann** and **Thomas Lang**, whose highly complex, technical approach created a breathtaking marriage of man and machine.

Rock'n'Roll Drumming in the 21st Century

At the time of this writing, fifty years have passed since rock'n'roll was officially christened as a definitive musical genre. In that time, the world's musical landscape has changed significantly. In addition to music programming, other technologies like music downloading and file sharing continue to radically alter the way that people access, listen to and even think about their music.

Through it all, rock has proven to be remarkably resilient. The rebellious spirit that has been its hallmark for fifty years reverberates undeterred as the music continues to be embraced by each new generation. And rock has been amazingly adaptable, evolving to include the latest trends and technologies without ever losing its core conception. Today's rock'n'roll is tremendously diverse, and with myriad hybrids like soft rock, nerd rock, kraut rock, shoegazer, grindcore, black metal, riot grrl and emo, some aspect of the music is guaranteed to appeal to every age group, every personality, every mood.

Rock'n'roll drumming has demonstrated a similar tenacity. Rock's rhythmic legacies - the backbeat, the straight eighth groove, the heavy emphasis of kick and snare – have become the underpinnings of countless other styles of music, and beats inspired by rock'n'roll can be found in the pop music of nearly every country in the world. Although some have posited that the latest influx of technology threatens the very existence of the drummer altogether, it seems that in a style like rock - which depends as much upon theatrics as it does on substance – such a scenario would be counterproductive. Instead, rock drummers will likely face a future in which they must continue to integrate their craft with the ever-shifting influence of technology, while simultaneously pushing the envelope to express themselves as artists.

See next page for endnotes and other sources for further study.

Long Live Rock'n'Roll!

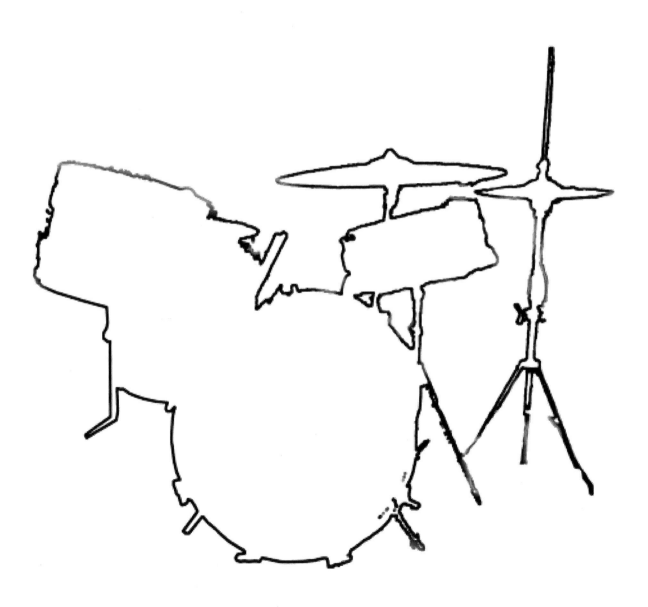

Endnotes:

1. Dawson, Jim and Steve Propes, *What Was the First Rock'n'Roll Record?*, Faber and Faber, 1992, p. xi
2. Louie Bellson – In an interview with the author, July 25, 2000.
3. *Backbeat*, p. 91.
4. Shaw, Arnold, *Honkers and Shouters: The Golden Years of Rhythm & Blues*, Collier Books, 1978, p. 35
5. Quincy Jones quote from the liner notes for *Jesse Stone: Alias Charles "Chuck" Calhoun*, (Bear Family, 1996).
6. Remo Belli – In an interview with the author, August 8, 2000.
7. Ventura, Robert, *Shadow Dancing in the U.S.A.*, Jeremy P. Tarcher, 1986, p. 157.
8. Unterburger, Ritchie – From the www.allmusic.com essay on the Beatles.
9. Weinberg, Max – pp. 179-80
10. All Music Guide, www.allmusic.com essay on Heavy Metal (author unlisted).
11. All Music Guide, www.allmusic.com essay on Fusion (author unlisted).

Sources:

Belsito, Peter and Bob Davis, *Hardcore California: A History of Punk and New Wave*. Berkeley: Last Gasp, 1983.

Blaine, Hal with David Goggin, *Hal Blaine and the Wrecking Crew*. Emeryville, Mix Books, 1990.

Dawson, Jim and Steve Propes, *What Was the First Rock'n'Roll Record*. Boston and London: Faber and Faber, 1992.

Graff, Gary and Daniel Durchholz (eds), *MusicHound Rock, The Essential Album Guide*. Detroit and London: Visible Ink Press, 1999.

Otfinoski, Steve, *The Golden Age of Rock Instrumentals*. New York: Billboard Books, 1997.

Palmer, Earl with Tony Sherman, *Backbeat: Earl Palmer's Story*. Washington and London: Smithsonian, 1999.

Shaw, Arnold, *Honkers and Shouters: The Golden Years of Rhythm & Blues*. New York: Collier Books, 1978.

Ventura, Robert, *Shadow Dancing in the U.S.A.* New York: Penguin Publications/Jeremy P. Tarcher, 1986.

Weinberg, Max, *The Big Beat: Conversations With Rock's Great Drummers*. New York: Contemporary Books, 1984.

Welch, Chris and Geoff Nicholls, *John Bonham: A Thunder of Drums*. San Francisco: Backbeat Books, 2001.